Meats
and
Sauces

Madame Benoit

Encyclopedia of microwave cooking

Meats and Sauces

Héritage+plus

Canadian Cataloguing in Publication Data

Benoit, Jehane, 1904-
  Meats and sauces

(Encyclopedia of microwave cooking)
(Héritage+plus)
Issued also in French under title: Les viandes
  et leurs sauces.
Includes index.
ISBN 2-7625-5803-4

1. Microwave cookery. 2. Cookery (Meat).
3. Sauces. I. Title. II. Series. III. Series:
Héritage+plus.

TX832.B45313 1985   641.5'882   C85-090171-5

First photo front: Country Casserole (p. 64)
          back top: Monique's Meat Loaf (p. 39)
       back Bottom: Greek Stephato (p. 29)
Last photo front: Orange-glazed Ham Steak (p. 80)
          back top: Sausages, scrambled eggs and browned potatoes (p. 85)
       back Bottom: Roast of Pork with Sauerkraut (p. 77)

Front cover design: Philippe Bouvry, graphic artist, designer
Front cover and inside photography: Paul Casavant
Conception and research: Marie-Christine Payette
Dishes loaned by courtesy of: Eaton, downtown, Montreal
  and of Le Curio, Montenach Mall, Beloeil.

Legal Deposits: 1st quarter 1985
Bibliothèque nationale du Québec
National Library of Canada

ISBN: 2-7625-5803-4   Printed in Canada

LES ÉDITIONS HÉRITAGE INC.
300, Arran, Saint-Lambert, Quebec J4R 1K5
(514) 672-6710

Table of contents

Foreword

Be Knowledgeable About Microwave Terms
There are many brands of microwave ovens on the market. That is why it is important to understand the language. Read and learn the following notes and microwave cooking will become clear and easy.

High or Full Power
This means a continuous cycle with maximum (100%) output, whatever your brand of oven.
The recipes in each volume of this encyclopedia were prepared for microwave ovens with wattage in the 650 - 700 range. If your oven has a lower output, increase the cooking time slightly according to the conversion chart.

All recipes in this book have been tested in a 650 and a 700-Watt microwave oven.
However, if you are using an oven with less wattage here is a comparative chart which will permit you to adjust the cooking time.

650-700W	500-600W	400-500W
15 seconds	18 seconds	21 seconds
30 seconds	36 seconds	42 seconds
45 seconds	54 seconds	1 minute
1 minute	1 min. 10 sec.	1 min. 25 sec.
2 minutes	2 min. 30 sec.	2 min. 45 sec.
3 minutes	3 min. 30 sec.	4 minutes
4 minutes	4 min. 45 sec.	5 min. 30 sec.
5 minutes	6 minutes	7 minutes
6 minutes	7 min. 15 sec.	8 min. 25 sec.
7 minutes	8 min. 25 sec.	9 min. 45 sec.
8 minutes	9 min. 30 sec.	11 minutes
9 minutes	10 min. 45 sec.	12 min. 30 sec.
10 minutes	12 minutes	14 minutes
15 minutes	18 minutes	20 minutes
20 minutes	24 minutes	27 minutes
25 minutes	30 minutes	34 minutes
30 minutes	36 minutes	41 minutes

This chart gives you an idea of the time needed for any food you cook in an oven with the above wattage.
However, it is always wise, regardless of wattage, to check the cooking when 2 minutes of the cooking period still remain. That's assuming, of course, that the cooking time indicated is over 2 minutes.

Let Stand
Many recipes read "Let stand. . . minutes after cooking". Since the microwave process of cooking is actually intense molecular vibration, food continues to cook even after the microwave energy is turned off. In a way, the same happens when food is cooked in x time in an ordinary oven and we let it stand.
With microwaves the standing time lets the molecules come to rest. This is just like a bouncing ball that dribbles down to a gradual stopping point. It is often referred to as "aftercook".
When a recipe says "Let stand x minutes, stir and serve," that is exactly what is meant.

Rotate

If your oven has a turntable or a special system, such as Rotaflow, or the microwave oven over the stove which has a hidden turntable that does the same work as the rotating type, then you do not have to rotate the dish in which the food is cooking. Otherwise, give a quarter turn to the dish once or twice during the cooking period.

Microwave-proof Dishes or Utensils

All dishes and utensils suitable for microwave cooking (e.g.: Pyrex, Corning, Micro-Dur, Earthenware casseroles, etc.).

Elevate

This term is most often used for meats. It means placing the roast or chicken, etc., on a rack or an inverted saucer to allow cooking juices to drain off from under the meat.
After microwaving a roast, allow meat to cool slightly, still on a rack to allow surface air to cool it evenly.
Another example: when making muffins or cupcakes, cool for at least 10 minutes, on a rack, to allow air to cool the food evenly.

Variable Power

This describes the choice of power levels that allow you to prepare food in the microwave which normally would be over sensitive to continuous microwave activity. To easily understand this process, it is actually an "on and off" cycle timed for varying amounts of microwave energy, which means that this pulsating action effectively creates slower cooking activity, without your having to worry about it. If your recipe calls for 1/2 power, this equals MEDIUM-LOW, which is like constant simmering.
When microwave cooking first began, ovens had only "Cook" and "Defrost" cycles. Some of you may still have these ovens, so remember that you effectively "simmer" on the Defrost cycle or whenever 1/2 power or MEDIUM is called for. For all other cooking, use the Cook cycle and add a few minutes to the cooking period called for in the recipe.

Temperature Probe

A thermometer-like, heat sensoring device to measure internal temperature of food during microwaving. Use only the "Probe" designed for your oven. It is perfect to cook a roast, by inserting the "Probe" in the meat, connecting it to the oven, then choosing the number referring to the cooking you wish to have; (e.g.: for a rare or well done roast, cook at the line printed on the oven time board and touch number indicated, then oven will start the cooking and at one point will give the degree of temperature needed to have the meat cooked according to your taste). You never have to worry how long it should take, since your oven will do it for you, and to perfection. Prepare the roast according to the recipe you are following.

Note : Never use a conventional thermometer in the microwave oven. There are many other ways to cook in the microwave, so always be ready to give serious attention to your oven manual, and you will soon find it is all very easy.

Introduction

In the course of time, many changes and modifications have taken place with regard to the preparation and cooking of food, table setting, and the time spent at such tasks. What a journey, going back to the time of the wood stove, which was still part of our daily life, even up to the years 1915 and 1920. Then, suddenly, important changes took place, gas and electricity for cooking, bringing about new kitchen equipment, new methods, savings in time, cleaning made easier, and not the least. . . white and elegant new stoves.

And now! A further gigantic step, which is changing and will continue to change many things... microwave ovens!

You buy a microwave oven, put it in the car, bring it home, place it on the kitchen counter, plug it in, and it's ready for use! And it's so easy for everyone to cook their favorite dishes in a microwave oven.

I, myself, started with the wood stove, and the memory still lingers on of those large slices of homemade bread toasted on top of the stove, and savored with fresh churned butter, homemade jam and café au lait with whole milk. What a delight! Of course, at that time, there was someone to rise à 5 a.m. to light the stove, and in the evening to rake over the ashes. There was a cook to churn the milk and make butter, and who spent innumerable summer hours making all that delicious jam.

Then followed the advent of the gas stove, with its coin-operated meter. If you forgot to feed in those 25¢ pieces, the gas was turned off! Still, it was an improvement over the wood stove. And one day the electric stove made an appearance. . . a miracle! We had seen nothing yet!

Modern technology has brought comfort, ease of work, perfection in cooking, the possibility of retaining the full flavor of food, the incredible reduction in hours of work, and the feasibility for each member of the family to cook his or her own meal, which gives the working mother a freedom she had never known before. This has been my experience: I cook more than ever before, yet my time spent in the kitchen has been reduced considerably. After thirteen years of cooking with microwave ovens, now I couldn't live without one. I have come to realize that you cannot know the true flavor of a vegetable or fish until you cook it in a microwave oven. And I can assure you that you need not learn a whole new cooking method, but simply learn to adapt your cooking to the microwave oven.

Many people have said to me: "I would not have the patience to change all my recipes", and so, I have decided to write this Encyclopedia of Microwave Cooking, so that you may realize how easy this method is once understood.

Microwave cooking is equally convenient for the small family with everyone working outside, as it is for the large family where larger servings are needed. All that's needed is knowing how to proceed.

The importance of knowing your oven

There are many models of microwave ovens, even of the same brand. It is therefore of utmost importance to become well acquainted with your oven, and to know and understand all its features.

What to do

- Once the oven is plugged in, place a bowl of water in it, close the door, and read the operation manual following every step as suggested.
  Example: Heat oven at HIGH for 2 minutes.

Look for Power Select HIGH and program, then look for the START setting; touch to put the oven on. You will then understand how this operation works.

Repeat this procedure for all types of operations, and very soon you will realize how easy it is, and you will understand how your own oven works.

Degree of Moisture in Food

(1) The degree of moisture in food:
    the higher it is: faster and shorter cooking period. — e.g.: spinach;
    the lower it is: slower and longer cooking period. — e.g.: carrots.
(2) The quantity of liquid added to the food:
    the greater the quantity, the longer the cooking period will be.
(3) The density of produce:
    Porous = faster cooking: tomatoes, spinach, mushrooms, etc.
    More dense = longer cooking: peas, lentils, etc.
(4) Room temperature is the ideal temperature to start cooking:
    Warmer temperature = faster cooking with food at room temperature;
    Colder temperature = longer cooking with food taken from refrigerator or after thawing.
(5) The structure of the food:
    Smaller pieces = faster cooking: a small potato;
    Larger pieces = slower cooking: a large potato.
(6) Often foods are covered during the cooking period to prevent the natural moisture from evaporating because the water in these foods has been activated.
(7) The degree of sugar content determines the degree of heat produced:
    The more sugar, the more intense the heat and the shorter the cooking period: syrup, caramel, etc.
(8) The more fat in food, the faster it will cook.
(9) The arrangement of the food plays an important role:
    4 to 5 potatoes placed in a circle will cook faster than if they were simply placed in the oven.

Degree of moisture - adding of water - density - thickness - structure - covers - amount of sugar - degree of fat - arrangement of food - appropriate accessories - are all key words relating your cooking to the factors of heat, weight and temperature.

How to cook food in the Microwave Oven

Microwaves are a form of high frequency radio wave similar to those used by a radio including AM, FM, and CB.
Electricity is converted into microwave energy by the magnetron tube, and microwaves are approximately four to six inches (10 to 15 cm) long with a diameter of about one-fourth inch (6mm). From the magnetron tube, microwave energy is transmitted to the oven cavity where it is: reflected, transmitted and absorbed.

Reflection
Microwaves are reflected by metal just as a ball is bounced off a wall. That is why the inside of the oven is metal covered with epoxy. A combination of stationary (interior walls) and rotating metal (turntable or stirrer fan) helps assure that the microwaves are well distributed within the oven cavity to produce even cooking.

Transmission
Microwaves pass through some materials such as paper, glass and plastic much like sunlight shining through a window. Because these substances do not absorb or reflect the microwave energy, they are ideal materials for microwave oven cooking containers.

Absorption
During heating, microwaves will be absorbed by food. They penetrate to a depth of about 3/4 to 1½ inches (2 to 4 cm). Microwave energy excites the molecules in the food (especially water, fat and sugar molecules), and causes them to vibrate at a rate of 2,450,000,000 times per second. This vibration causes friction, and heat is produced. If you vigorously rub your hands together, you will feel heat produced by friction. The internal cooking is then done by conduction. **The heat** which is produced by friction is conducted to the center of the food.

Foods also continue to cook by conduction during standing time, which keeps the cooked food warm for 4 to 10 minutes after cooking, and makes it possible to cook 3 to 4 dishes with only one oven, and to serve everything warm.

Example: If your menu calls for a roast, potatoes and green peas, cook the roast first. During its waiting period, cook the potatoes, they will remain warm from 20 to 30 minutes covered with a cloth, then the vegetable with the shortest cooking period.

The dessert may be cooked before the meat, or if it is to be served hot, cook it during the meal and let it stand in the oven. The oven goes off when the bell rings, and the food may be left inside until it is time to serve it.

Cooking equipment

Microwave cooking opens new possibilities in convenience and flexibility for cooking containers. There are new microwave accessories constantly being introduced, but do not feel you need to purchase all new equipment. You will be surprised at the numerous items you already have in your kitchen that are suitable for microwave cooking.

Glass, Ceramic and China

Most of these utensils are excellent for use in the microwave oven. Many manufacturers now identify microwave oven safe dishes. Heat resistant glassware, unless it has metallic trim or decoration, can most always be used. However, be careful about using delicate glassware since it may crack, not from microwave energy, but from the heat of the food.

Here are a few heat-resistant glass cookware items I find invaluable in microwave cookery. You probably have many of these items on your shelf already:

- glass measuring cups
- custard cups
- mixing bowls
- loaf dish
- covered casserole dishes
- oblong baking dish, non-metallic
- cake dishes, round or square, glass
- pie plate, plastic, glass or ceramic
- large bowls, 8 to 10 cups (2 to 2.5 L), with covers
- cake dishes, round, long, square, Pyrex, plastic, "Micro-Dur".

Browning Dish (Corning)

There are two sizes: 8 x 8 x 2 inches (21 x 21 x 5 cm) — 6 cups (1.5 L)
9.5 x 9.5 x 2 inches (24 x 24 x 5 cm) — 10 cups (2.5 L)

There is also a Browning Grill: 8 x 8 inches (21 x 21 cm).

A Browning Dish has a special dielectric coating on the underside. The coating is activated by preheating (uncovered) the empty Browning Dish for no more than 7 minutes for the smaller one or 9 minutes for the larger one or for the grill in the Microwave.

Do not remove dish from oven after preheating, simply place in the preheated dish the steak, or whatever you wish to brown, pressing down on the food with a fork to obtain perfect contact with the bottom of the dish. If the recipe calls for oil or butter or other fat, it must be added after preheating the dish. Brown 5 to 7 minutes or according to recipe. You will be surprised how well browned the food will be. Turn it and let stand in the dish in the Microwave the time it took to brown the bottom part, without heat, as giving it more cooking time will only dry the food. It is then ready to serve.

A Browning Dish can be an extremely handy accessory with many uses: to brown steaks and chops, etc., stir-fry vegetables, cook omelets, reheat pizzas, grill sandwiches, and much more.

Do not limit these items to being browners only! They are just as useful as regular microwave cookware. Without preheating, the base will not get hot so can be used for microwaving vegetables, casseroles, desserts, fish, etc. The Browning Dish cover is used more frequently for this type of cooking.

Browning Dishes are for use in Microwaves only, and not in regular ovens (coating could be scratched by oven racks), or on range top as possible damage to special coating could result.

Do not use Probe with the Browning Dish.

Cooking bags

Cooking bags designed to withstand boiling, freezing or conventional heating are safe to use in the microwave oven. Make six small slits in the top of the bag to allow steam to escape. If you use twist-ties to close the bag, make sure the ends are completely rolled around the bag, not loose, as they could act as an antenna and cause arcing (blue sparks). It is better to use a piece of cotton string or a nylon tie, or a strip cut from the open end of the bag. DO NOT COOK FOOD IN BROWN OR WHITE PAPER BAGS.

Plastic wrap

Plastic wrap such as Saran Wrap™ and others can be used to cover dishes in most recipes. Over an extended heating time, some disfiguration of the wrap may occur. When using plastic wrap as a casserole dish cover, fold back a small section of plastic wrap from the edge of the dish to allow some steam to escape. When removing plastic wrap "covers", as well as any glass lid, be careful to remove it away from you to avoid steam burns. After heating, loosen plastic but let dish stand covered. Please note that it is not always necessary to cover all foods.

Food Covering for Sensor Cooking

When cooking by Sensor method an inch (2.5 cm) of water is needed in the bottom of the dish and the dish must be covered with plastic wrap. The Microwave-safe plastic dish "MICRO-DUR" does not need the plastic wrap as its cover keeps the steam inside the dish.

Aluminum foil

Aluminum foil can be used safely when certain guidelines are followed. Because it reflects microwave energy, foil can be used to advantage in some cases. Small pieces of foil are used to cover areas such as the tips of chicken wings, chicken legs, or roasts that cook more quickly than the rest. Foil is used in these cases to slow or stop the cooking process and prevent overcooking. The strips of foil placed on the edges of a roast or the ends of chicken legs can be removed halfway through the cooking period.

Food characteristics

Food characteristics which affect conventional cooking are more pronounced with microwave heating.

Size and quantity

Microwave cooking is faster than cooking with gas or electricity, therefore the size and quantity of food play an important role in cooking time.

Shape

Uniform sizes heat more evenly. To compensate for irregular shapes, place thin pieces toward the center of the dish and thicker pieces toward the edge of the dish.

Bone and fat

Both affect heating. Bones conduct heat and cause the meat next to it to be heated more quickly*. Large amounts of fat absorb microwave energy and meat next to these areas may overcook.

*See Aluminum foil paragraph.

Starting temperature

Room temperature foods take less time to heat than refrigerator or frozen foods.

Spacing

Individual foods, such as baked potatoes and hors d'oeuvres, will heat more evenly if placed in the oven equal distances apart. When possible, arrange foods in a circular pattern.
Similarly, when placing foods in a baking dish, arrange around the outside of dish, not lined up next to each other. Foods should NOT be stacked on top of each other.

Stirring
Stirring is often necessary during microwave cooking. Recipes advise as to frequency of stirring.

Example: *Always bring the cooked outside edges toward the center and the less cooked center portions toward the outside. Some foods should be turned in the container during heating.*

Standing time
Most foods will continue to cook by conduction after the microwave oven is turned off. In meat cookery, the internal temperature will rise 5°F to 15°F if allowed to stand, covered, for 10 to 20 minutes. Casseroles and vegetables need a shorter amount of standing time, but this standing time is necessary to allow foods to complete cooking in the center without overcooking on the edges.

Power Select Settings
Some microwave ovens are equipped with multiple Power Select settings: HIGH, MEDIUM-HIGH, MEDIUM, MEDIUM-LOW, DEFROST, LOW, WARM, and DELAY/STAND.
While most foods can be heated on HIGH (full power), certain types of foods, milk for example, will benefit from heating with a reduced amount of energy over a slightly longer time.
This variety of settings offers you complete flexibility in microwave cooking.

IMPORTANT

The following recipes were tested in 650 — 700 watts microwave ovens.

Lower-wattage ovens may necessitate some adjustment in timing. (See chart on page 9.)

The recipes in general will serve 6 medium portions or 4 large portions.

Power Level Chart

Power	Output	Use
HIGH	100% .... (700 watts)	Boil water Brown ground meat Cook fresh fruits and vegetables Cook fish Cook poultry (up to 3 lb [1.5 kg]) Heat beverages (not containing milk) Make candy Preheat Browning Dish (accessory)
MEDIUM-HIGH	90% .... (650 watts)	Heat frozen foods (not containing eggs or cheese) Heat canned foods Reheat leftovers Warm baby food
MEDIUM	70% .... (490 watts)	Bake cakes Cook meats Cook shellfish Prepare eggs and delicate food
MEDIUM-LOW	50% .... (360 watts)	Bake muffins Cook custards Melt butter and chocolate Prepare rice
LOW	27% .... (200 watts)	Less tender cuts of meat Simmer stews and soups Soften butter and cheese
WARM	10% .... (70 watts)	Keep foods at serving temperature Rise yeast breads Soften ice cream
"Defrost"	35% .... (245 watts)	All thawing, see Defrosting Charts
"Delay Stand"	0% .... (0 watts)	Start heating at later time Program stand time after cooking

IMPI — International Microwave Power Institute — is an international institution governing microwave data throughout the world for kitchens, hospitals, etc.
IMPI have set the standards which have been adopted with regard to the designation of Power Settings for Microwave Ovens: HIGH, MEDIUM-HIGH, MEDIUM, MEDIUM-LOW, LOW, REHEAT, DEFROST, START, which must be observed everywhere in the world.

Roast Beef (p. 27) →

The Turntable

It is to our advantage to study and make use of the innovative technologies in microwave ovens, as they always make it easier for us. Do make sure to read the instructions in your oven manual to learn about and understand the various cooking methods your oven has to offer and their use.

The following are some features which you need to acquaint yourself with in order to take full advantage of them.

Magnetic Turntable

Some ovens are equipped with an automatic magnetic turntable or a small fan in the top of the oven, or an invisible rotating system (whichever is featured in your Microwave, it will be explained in your instruction manual), then you do not have to rotate the dish.

If your Microwave has neither turntable, nor fan, nor invisible rotating system, then you will have to rotate the dish for even cooking as the Microwave may tend to focus more on a definite spot in the food, especially if there is fat in the meat, and remember that they are not always visible. What happens is that the fat parts cook more quickly because the reflection area is not altered, so, of course the cooking dish may be rotated.

Auto Sensor Cooking

The Auto Sensor is yet another wonder of Microwave cooking! The Microwave oven determines the cooking time. You wish to cook either a vegetable, meat, poultry, stew, etc., and are wondering what cooking time to allow. Relax.

If your Microwave features Auto Sensor Cooking it will be indicated on the oven panel with a COOK or INSTA-MATIC, etc. section, and your oven manual will give you instructions as to its use.

Numbers 1 to 7 or 8 are also shown on the panel, each one indicating the type of food for cooking, e.g. A7 Soft Vegetables (brussels sprouts, zucchini, etc.); A8 Hard Vegetables (carrots, etc.) Always refer to your oven manual for precise instructions.

There are two important points to remember when cooking by Auto Sensor (COOK). Whatever the food, a little water must always be added, from 1/4 to 1/3 cup (60 - 80 mL), depending on the quantity, and the dish must be well covered with either plastic wrap or a tight-fitting lid that will hold securely in place throughout the cooking period. There are some dishes, of various shapes and sizes, with a perfect lid for Auto Sensor Cooking which are available on the market. They are called "Micro-Dur".

- It is important that the oven door not be opened during the cooking period. The operation takes place in two stages.
- The selected number appears and remains in the display window until such time as the steam is detected by the humidity sensor, which is inside the oven. At this time a BEEP is heard and the cooking time appears in the display window.

If your oven does not have a turntable, you will have to give a quarter of a turn to the dish, whatever the food, once or twice during cooking.

A few hints for defrosting meats

- Defrost in original wrapper (not in foil), by placing meat in a dish to prevent liquid from running.
- Set Power Select at DEFROST and heat for time recommended in following chart.
- Turn food over two or three times during the defrosting cycle.
- Before preparing food, let it stand for a time equal to the defrost time.
- Rinse under cold water to remove all remaining ice particles.

← Top: Broiled Steak, Madeira Sauce (p. 31)
← Bottom: Red Wine Rib Roast (p. 29)

Defrost Chart		Approx. Defrosting Time (minutes per pound) at Power Select DEFROST	Standing Time (minutes per pound)
Beef			
Roast	Tenderloin	5 to 6	5 to 6
	Chuck or rump	5 to 6	5 to 6
	Sirloin, rolled	5 to 6	5 to 6
Steak			
	Boneless sirloin	6 to 7	6 to 7
	Flank	4 to 5	4 to 5
Miscellaneous			
	Frankfurters	5 to 6	5 to 6
	Ground beef*	5 to 6	5 to 6
	Liver	5 to 6	5 to 6

* **Note:** *When defrosting ground beef, halfway through heating remove outer portions of beef (thawed) to prevent cooking of edges before center is completely thawed.*

Weight defrost

Certain ovens have a choice of defrosting by weight or defrosting by time-defrost method. You can use your weight defrost method which is very accurate by first reading the directions given in your operation manual. Weight Defrost is based on the following automated cycle. Defrost Cycle for Meats and Poultry Pieces goes between 0.1 lb (approximately 1½ oz.) and 5.9 lb. By touching the weight and defrost pads of your oven control panel, the automatic count-up system will indicate in the display window the weight from 1 to 6 lb (0.5 to 3 kg) of such common meat and poultry items that are usually defrosted.

Again I would like to repeat, if your oven has this automatic weight defrost make sure you read the instructions given in your oven manual so it will be fully understood.

A few hints for reheating food in the Microwave Oven

Like defrosting, reheating a wide variety of foods is a highly appreciated use of a microwave oven. It not only saves time, money and clean-up, but most foods reheat so well that there is little loss of taste. Leftovers take on that "just cooked" flavor which has never been possible when reheating by conventional methods. Many foods are actually better when reheated because they have had time to allow the flavors to blend.

Such foods as spaghetti sauce, lasagna, mashed potatoes, creams, stews are examples of foods whose flavor improves with reheating.

A plate of food

Arrange foods on a microwave-safe plate with thicker or denser portions towards the rim of the plate. Add gravy or butter where desired. Cover plate with waxed paper, reheat at MEDIUM-HIGH for 2 to 3 minutes, checking after 2 minutes.

To reheat by Sensor

Prepare plate in the same manner, cover completely with plastic wrap, and touch pad 1 of Sensor or any other as instructed in your microwave manual, that is, of course, if you have a Sensor pad on your oven. The oven does the work. You do not have to determine the time.

Casseroles

Stir well and add a small amount of liquid (water, milk, consommé, gravy, etc.), usually 1/4 cup (60 mL) is sufficient, cover with a glass lid or plastic wrap. Again if your oven has a Sensor or Insta-matic Cooking Heat, touch pad 1 or as directed in your microwave manual.

To reheat by time

Cover with waxed paper and heat at MEDIUM-HIGH for 2 to 6 minutes, stirring halfway through heating.

Beef

Beef

Learn to know beef cuts

To cook a perfect browned roast, tender and juicy, whatever cooking method you select, you must first of all buy the perfect cut for the chosen cooking method.

There are, in beef as in other meats, the more tender and the less tender cuts. If your choice is braised or simmered or boiled roast, then you must buy the proper cut for that particular cooking.

Study the chart given below to understand which are the more tender and the less tender cuts.

Examples: A loin roast, either porterhouse or wing roast, a fine and very tender cut, but also more expensive, will give a first class roast beef.

The eye of round, sirloin point, which is the tender cut in the hip, as well as the cross rib, the tender cut in the shoulder, are very good roasts and the cost is not as high.

However, a cross rib must be 4 to 5 inches (10 to 12.5 cm) thick for a perfect roast. It is best to braise or boil a thinner cut.

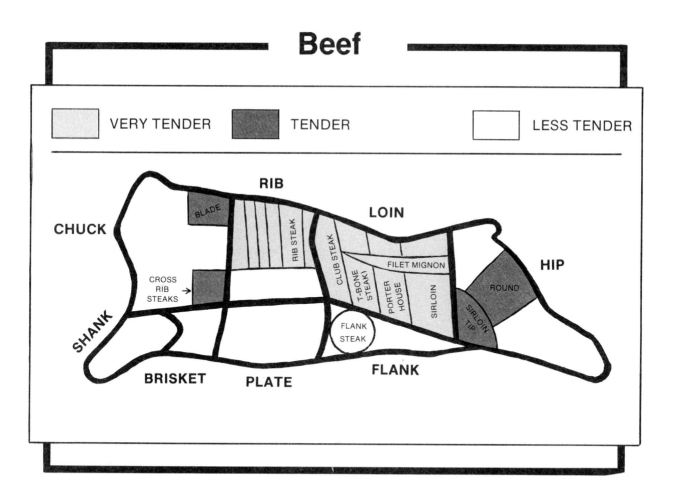

Tenderizing less tender beef and other meat cuts

There are meat cuts, whether beef, pork or veal, which are less tender and cost much less. They may be marinated in many ways, which not only makes the meat more tender but also gives it an interesting flavor.

1. Beat steaks or meat cubes for stewing with a wooden or metal mallet, which tenderizes the meat fibers. That is the principle of tenderized steaks sold by the butcher, but it costs less to do it yourself. Very good mallets with a metal tip are found in kitchen specialty shops.
2. Baste a thin slice of meat with a mixture of vegetable oil and fresh lemon juice. For a steak, 1 tablespoon (15 mL) each of oil and lemon juice will do. Cover and marinate from a minimum of 30 minutes to 12 hours, refrigerated.
3. My favorite method to tenderize meat cubes for stews is to cover with buttermilk or yogurt, mix well, cover and let stand 12 hours, refrigerated. Before using, drain thoroughly, wipe each cube with absorbent paper.
4. For a braised roast, the French marinade is the best. Place in a 4-cup (1 L) measure 1 cup (250 mL) of red wine, 2 cups (500 mL) water, 1 onion, peeled and sliced, 2 peeled garlic cloves, 1 teaspoon (5 mL) marinating spices or 1/2 teaspoon (2 mL) each savory and thyme, 1 teaspoon (5 mL) brown sugar or molasses, 10 peppercorns. Heat 2 minutes at HIGH. Let stand 20 minutes. Pour over the meat, coat well with the mixture, cover and let stand 24 hours.
5. **Mexican Marinade** — In Mexico, meats are not tender; they must be marinated. Here is one of their best marinating mixtures: it is not economical, but it gives the meat a perfect flavor. Peel an avocado and crush the green pulp with a fork, add the juice of one lemon or lime, 2 garlic cloves, finely minced. Baste the meat pieces with this mixture, cover and let marinate in the refrigerator for 12 to 24 hours.
6. **French marinade** — This one will keep 6 to 8 weeks in a well-covered glass jar in the refrigerator. In the provinces, fresh grape juice is used, which I have replaced successfully with unsweetened grape juice (Welsh).

>   **2/3 cup (160 mL) minced onion**
>   **3/4 cup (200 mL) diced celery with leaves**
>   **1/3 cup (80 mL) cider vinegar**
>   **1/2 cup (125 mL) vegetable oil**
>   **1 cup (250 mL) grape juice**
>   **1 tbsp. (15 mL) Worcestershire sauce**
>   **1/2 tsp. (2 mL) salt**
>   **1/2 tsp. (2 mL) garlic powder or**
>   **3 garlic cloves, finely minced**

Mix all the ingredients together, and refrigerate in a glass jar. Use as a marinating mixture, pouring it over the meat and letting it stand for 12 hours, covered and refrigerated.

Roasting Methods in the Microwave

There are many roasting methods for meats. Depending on the model of your microwave oven, there may be one or several.

Your oven operation manual will advise you as to what roasting methods are available.

Meat cooking by Microwave

The cooking of meats in the microwave oven allows for quick and easy preparation of a number of meats, whether they are roasted, braised or boiled.

1. Meat temperature before cooking: room temperature is desirable. If the meat is just out of the refrigerator, extend the cooking time.
2. Shape and size of piece.
3. Tenderness of cut and desired degree of doneness.

Place a microwave rack or an inverted saucer or glass cover under the roast, fat side down, to prevent its steeping in its juice. Give the roast half a turn during the cooking period, as well as the dish. If juice accumulates in the dish, remove it and reserve for making gravy. This is important, as the juice absorbs energy and prevents the meat from cooking to perfection. If the roast falls over, prop it up with an inverted dessert cup.

Meats can be shielded at the beginning of cooking or halfway through cooking with aluminum foil. Tips of bones in a roast beef should be shielded with a 2-inch (5 cm) wide strip of foil.

Tips of rolled roasts should also be shielded. If you wish to shield only at the beginning, remove foil halfway through the cooking.

Note: Meat continues to cook after being removed from the oven. Cover it and let it stand 15 to 20 minutes.

Convection cooking

Convection cooking with the microwave oven gives excellent results just like an electric convection stove, with the constant circulation of hot and dry air blown around the food being cooked. Temperature is set as required by the recipe — i.e. 300°F, 350°F, 400°F (150°C, 180°C, 200°C).

Take advantage of this cooking method to roast your meats as you would normally do. They will be browned to perfection and cooked to your taste. If your oven has an automatic turntable, the cooking and browning will always be very even.

Besides, convection cooking allows you to use all your favorite recipes, normally cooked in your electric or gas stove, without any change in the cut or cooking time required.

Cooking by temperature probe

When the probe is inserted into the food, it controls the internal temperature.

As soon as the selected temperature is reached, the unit will automatically be turned off. The probe will also help to hold the food until serving at the final cooking temperature, for time set at Temperature HOLD.

I use this method often because it gives perfect results; the temperature probe measures the food temperature precisely and it is cooked to your taste. If I wish to have a roast cooked rare or medium or well done, I program according to my needs, by touch control. The temperature probe will sense the internal temperature of the food and will turn the unit off automatically.

In the following recipes, you will find meats cooked according to one of the methods.

The temperature probe: helpful information

1. Insert the probe at least one inch (2.5 cm) into the food and plug it to the oven.
2. Always insert probe into meat in a horizontal position.
3. Poke probe through plastic wrap into center of food when food is covered, in a horizontal position.
4. Do NOT use the probe with frozen foods or the browning dish (Corning).
5. Remove probe from oven cavity receptacle with oven mitts to avoid burns.
6. Clean probe with mild detergent and a soft cloth, if necessary. DO NOT immerse in water or wash in dishwater.
7. Store probe in its original container.

DO NOT USE A CONVENTIONAL MEAT THERMOMETER IN FOOD WHILE HEATING IN THE MICROWAVE OVEN. However, a conventional meat thermometer may be used to check the internal temperature of a food item when removed from the oven.

Special Hints for Roasting Meats

- Place roast, cleaned and wiped dry, on microwave oven-safe roasting rack or inverted plate or glass cover in a baking dish.
- Season to taste. DO NOT SALT except for braised or boiled meats.
- Loosely cover dish with wax paper to prevent splattering.
- Set Power Select at HIGH or as required.
- Cover less meaty portions of meat with aluminum foil half way through cooking to prevent overcooking of these areas. Use wooden toothpicks to hold the foil in place.
- Check internal temperature of meat with a thermometer. DO NOT USE A CONVENTIONAL THERMOMETER IN MEAT WHILE IT IS IN THE OVEN.

- Let stand, covered, 10 to 15 minutes after cooking. This time allows the temperature to equalize throughout. The internal meat temperature will rise 5°F to 10°F (3°C to 6°C).

Roast Beef in the Microwave Oven

No matter what type of microwave oven you have, you will never fail to have a lovely browned and tender roast, cooked to your taste, rare, medium or well done, by following the instructions given below.

Before you start, study carefully the cooking chart for beef in the microwave oven, keeping in mind that the times apply only to meat at room temperature. If the meat cut is just out of the refrigerator, or has just been defrosted with no standing time (see meat defrosting), you must add 2 minutes per pound (500 g). Meat taken out of the refrigerator 1 or 2 hours before cooking, will be juicier and more tender and will brown better.

If you wish to roast a piece of meat that is frozen, follow the instructions given in your operation manual for Defrosting. However, once the roast has thawed, it is important to let it stand one hour at room temperature before roasting it.

Beef Roasting Chart for Microwave Oven

Rare — 120°F (55°C) — 8 minutes at HIGH for the first pound of roast weight.
8 minutes per pound at MEDIUM for remaining weight.

Example: A 3-lb (1.5 kg) roast should cook 8 minutes at HIGH and 16 minutes at MEDIUM.

Medium — 140°F (60°C) — 9 minutes at HIGH for the first pound of roast weight.
9 minutes per pound at MEDIUM for the remaining weight.

Well done — 160°F (70°C) — 9 minutes at HIGH for the first pound of roast weight.
11 to 12 minutes per pound at MEDIUM for remaining weight.

Bone-in Rib Roast
In the Microwave

To succeed with this cut, a browning dish (Corning) is a must, tips of the flat bones under the roast must be shielded with a strip of foil, as indicated in your operation manual.

A 4 to 6-lb (2 to 3 kg) loin or wing roast with bone

2 tsp. (10 mL) paprika

1 tsp. (5 mL) dry mustard

2 tbsp. (30 mL) soft butter or margarine

1 medium onion, cut in four

Cream the paprika, mustard and butter. Shield tips of the bones with a 2-inch (5 cm) strip of foil. Preheat browning dish 7 minutes at HIGH. Place the roast in the oven without removing dish from the oven, fat side down. Cook at HIGH 8 minutes.
Baste the raw parts of the meat with the creamed **mix**ture.
Place the roast on microwave rack or inverted saucer set in a baking dish, fat side up. Sprinkle with paprika. Do not salt. Place the onion pieces in the bottom of the dish. Cook at MEDIUM 8 minutes per pound (500 g). Remove foil after the first 8 minutes, then cook to your taste following the Beef Roasting Chart.
When the roast is cooked, place it on a serving dish and let stand 10 minutes, covered, in a warm place. Prepare the gravy to your taste, same as for Rolled Rib Roast, or according to the recipe you choose in the Sauce chapter.

Roast Beef *(photo opposite page 16)*
With Temperature Probe

If your oven has a temperature probe, that is the simple method to cook a roast to perfection, whatever the cut: cross rib, eye of round or rib roast, with bone or boneless.
See "Temperature Probe" paragraph for directions.
This method gives perfect results every time. The temperature probe will sense the internal temperature of food and will turn the unit off automatically when the programmed temperature is reached.

A 4 to 6-lb (2 to 3 kg) roast of your choice

1/2 tsp. (2 mL) ground pepper

1/2 tsp. (2 mL) paprika

1 tsp. (5 mL) dry mustard

1 garlic clove, chopped fine

1 bay leaf, broken up into small pieces

1 tbsp. (15 mL) vegetable oil

Mix together the pepper, paprika, mustard, garlic, bay leaf and vegetable oil. Spread over the raw parts of the meat.
Place the spatter shield in the oven tray, set the low rack over the shield, put a Pyrex or ceramic plate under the rack and place the meat on the rack. Insert the temperature probe in the meat and plug it to the oven. Then select the desired combination as indicated on your oven, according to how you wish your roast, rare, medium or well done. Set your oven and touch the chosen number. The temperature probe will sense the internal temperature of the meat and will turn off the unit automatically when the selected temperature is reached.

Remove the roast from the oven, remove the temperature probe and make the gravy with the juice accumulated in the bottom of the plate.
Proceed as for rolled rib roast in the microwave or make a sauce of your choice as in the Sauce chapter.

Rolled Rib Roast
Microwave cooking

Make sure there are no large pieces of fat inside the meat. However, a coat of fat on top will give the roast a better flavor. This roast is cooked without any salt.

A 4 to 5-lb (2 to 2.5 kg) loin or wing roast, boned and rolled

2 tbsp. (30 mL) vegetable oil or melted butter

1 tsp. (5 mL) paprika

1/2 tsp. (2 mL) thyme

1/2 tsp. (2 mL) fresh ground pepper

a small garlic clove, crushed

2 tbsp. (30 mL) very fine breadcrumbs

Mix together in a bowl the vegetable oil or melted butter, paprika, thyme, pepper, garlic and breadcrumbs. Baste the top fat and the sides of the roast with this mixture.
Place the roast on a microwave rack or an inverted saucer set in an 8 x 12-inch (20 x 30 cm) baking dish. Roast according to time given in the Beef Roasting Chart.
When cooked, let meat stand, covered, 10 to 15 minutes in a warm place.
To make the gravy, remove roast and rack from the baking dish. Add to the juice in the bottom of the dish, 1/4 cup (60 mL) of a liquid of your choice, cold tea or Madeira or sherry or red wine, and 1 teaspoon (5 mL) Dijon mustard. Mix well, crushing the tiny bits of caramel from the meat which give flavor and color to the meat juices. Heat 1 minute at HIGH when ready to serve.

To make a creamy gravy
Add to the fat 1 tablespoon (15 mL) flour. Mix well, cook 2 minutes at HIGH, stirring once. Add 1/2 cup (125 mL) of a liquid of your choice, as given previously. Should you choose Madeira or sherry, add only 1/4 cup (60 mL) plus 1/4 cup (60 mL) cold water. Stir well and cook 3 minutes at HIGH, stirring once.

Note: See Sauce chapter, for special sauces.

Roast Beef (photo opposite page 16)
Convection Method

This method is the same as in an electric stove. The beef cuts as already mentioned for the other cooking methods remain the same.
Here is the procedure to follow.
To cook a roast beef by convection, I recommend a Spencer or Rib Eye Roast or a Rib Roast, or for a more economical cut, a Cross Rib at least 4 to 5 inches (10 to 13 cm) thick.

A 3 to 5-lb (1.5 to 2.5 kg) roast beef

3 tbsp. (50 mL) of fat of your choice

1 tbsp. (15 mL) dry mustard

Cream the fat and mustard. Pat the roast dry with absorbent paper. Spread the mustard butter over the raw parts of the meat. Sprinkle paprika generously over the top fat. Place the spatter shield in the oven tray. Set the rack. Preheat oven to 350°F (180°C) for 15 minutes. Set a plate under the rack.
Place the roast on the rack, and cook 10 to 15 or 20 minutes per pound (500 g) at 350°F (180°C), whether you wish your roast to be rare, medium or well done. When the roast is cooked, make your gravy as for any other roast.

Three-Star Roast Beef
Convection Method

This superb roast is done by the convection method. If your microwave oven also has the convection method, do not hesitate to cook this roast, if you wish to serve a first-class roast when entertaining friends or for a special family celebration.

A 4 to 5-lb (2 to 2.5 kg) beef sirloin,
boned and rolled

3 tbsp. (50 mL) soft butter

2 tbsp. (30 mL) Dijon mustard

1 tbsp. (15 mL) dry mustard

2 tbsp. (30 mL) chili sauce

1/2 cup (125 mL) dry Madeira or sherry

1/2 cup (125 mL) beef consommé

Prepare the oven by placing the spatter shield in the oven ceramic tray, set the low rack over the shield. Preheat oven to 375°F (190°C).
Mix together the butter, Dijon mustard, dry mustard and chili sauce. Spread this mixture over the raw parts of the meat. Place a pie plate under the rack. Roast at 375°F (190°C) 15 to 20 minutes per pound (500 g), whether you wish your roast to be rare or medium. When cooked, place the roast on a warm plate and keep in a warm place. With a spoon, remove the fat floating on top of the gravy. To the remaining brown juice, add the wine of your choice or the consommé, scraping the plate to crush the brown particles. Heat 5 minutes at HIGH in the microwave, stirring twice during cooking.

Eye of round "à la Bordelaise"
Microwave Cooking

The eye of round or the sirloin are more economical beef cuts than the rib roast. This cooking method will result in deliciously tender meat. Serve with mashed potatoes or fine noodles topped with the meat gravy.

3 to 4 lb (1.5 to 2 kg) beef eye of round or siloin

1/3 cup (80 mL) olive or vegetable oil

1/2 cup (125 mL) red wine

1/2 cup (125 mL) beef broth

1 cup (125 mL) onions, thinly sliced

1/4 cup (60 mL) fresh parsley, minced

2 bay leaves

1 tsp. (5 mL) thyme

1 tsp. (5 mL) sugar

1 tsp. (5 mL) salt

1/2 tsp. (2 mL) peppercorns, coarsely ground

3 slices bacon

1 tbsp. (15 mL) wine or cider vinegar

Mix together in a large bowl, the oil, wine, beef broth, onions, parsley, bay leaves, thyme, sugar, salt and pepper. Roll the piece of meat in the mixture, cover and marinate 24 hours, refrigerated. Turn the piece of meat 2 to 3 times during that period.

To cook, place the bacon slices on a sheet of white paper. Cook 2 minutes at HIGH. Place in the bottom of a deep dish large enough to hold the piece of meat.

Remove meat from marinade. Drain, reserving the juice. Place the remaining onions and herbs in the strainer over the bacon. Set the meat on top and add 1 cup (250 mL) of the marinade juice. Cover and cook 10 minutes at HIGH, reduce power to MEDIUM and cook 40 to 70 minutes, or until the meat is tender.

When cooked, place the meat on a warm platter. Add to the sauce 1/4 cup (60 mL) of the remaining marinade juice and the spoonful of vinegar. Cook 5 minutes at HIGH. Serve in a sauceboat.

Broiled Steak with Mushrooms
Microwave Cooking

A steak of your choice

1 tsp. (5 mL) butter

1/2 tsp. (2 mL) tarragon

1 garlic clove, cut in two

1 to 2 cups (250 - 500 mL) mushrooms, thinly sliced

salt and pepper to taste

Broil the steak of your choice in the microwave, following the recipe for Broiled Steak, Madeira Sauce. When the steak has stood for 3 minutes, place it on a warm plate. To the cooking juice, add the butter, tarragon and garlic, and cook 1 minute at HIGH. Stir well. Add the mushrooms. Mix well together. Salt and pepper, then finish cooking at HIGH 3 minutes. Pour around steak.

Greek Stefatho *(first photo back bottom)*
Microwave Cooking

A meal in a dish, beef or lamb, eggplant and rice. In Greece, this is family fare. It may be cooked a day in advance, refrigerated, and reheated the following day, covered, either by Sensor "Cycle A-1" or 10 to 15 minutes at MEDIUM.

2-lb (1 kg) beef round, in 1-inch (2.5 cm) cubes

1/2 tsp. (2 mL) pepper

1 tsp. (5 mL) sugar

1 tsp. (5 mL) cinnamon

1/3 cup (80 mL) vegetable oil

12 small white onions

2 cups (500 mL) beef broth

A 7½ oz. (213 mL) can tomato sauce

1/4 cup (60 mL) vegetable oil

1 medium eggplant, peeled and diced

1 green pepper, cut in strips

1/2 cup (125 mL) long grain rice

Mix together in a plate the pepper, salt, sugar and cinnamon. Roll the beef cubes in the mixture. Heat the oil in a browning dish (Corning) 4 minutes at HIGH.

Add the meat cubes to the hot oil. Stir a few seconds and cook at MEDIUM-HIGH 4 minutes. Stir and cook another 4 minutes at MEDIUM-HIGH. Remove meat to a 8-cup (2 L) dish. Heat the remaining fat in the dish (there is very little), 1 minute at HIGH. Add the onions, cook 2 minutes at HIGH. Add 1/2 cup (125 mL) beef broth and tomato sauce. Mix well. Cover with casserole lid or plastic wrap. Cook 1 hour at MEDIUM, stirring after 30 minutes.

Heat the 1/4 cup (60 mL) oil 5 minutes in the browning dish (Corning). Add the eggplant, stir well. Cook 5 minutes at HIGH. Add the green pepper. Heat 1 minute at HIGH. Add to the casserole at the end of its cooking period, together with the rice and the remaining beef broth. Stir well. Cover and cook 20 to 25 minutes at MEDIUM-HIGH. Stir after 15 minutes of cooking.

Red Wine Rib Roast *(photo opposite page 17 bottom)*
Microwave Cooking

A rib roast "Provençale". A method which differs greatly from classic roasting. An ideal recipe for a buffet, to serve cold rib roast, thinly sliced.

A 3½ to 4-lb (1.5 to 2 kg) rib roast, boned and rolled

1/4 cup (60 mL) flour

1 tsp. (5 mL) paprika

4 tbsp. (60 mL) butter

1 cup (250 mL) onion, sliced

1/2 cup (125 mL) grated carrots

1 garlic clove, minced

2 tbsp. (30 mL) hot brandy

1 cup (250 mL) dry red wine

1 tsp. (5 mL) salt

1/2 tsp. (2 mL) fresh ground pepper

1 bay leaf

1/2 tsp. (2 mL) thyme

Pat the roast dry with absorbent paper and roll it in the flour and paprika spread out on waxed paper to cover the meat completely.

Preheat a browning dish (Corning) or a "caquelon" (Panasonic) 8 minutes at HIGH. Place the butter in the hot dish without removing it from the oven. When the butter has melted, which occurs very quickly, place the roast in the dish fat side down. Cook 2 minutes at HIGH, turn the roast and cook another 2 minutes at HIGH, repeat this operation for the two other sides.

Remove roast from the dish. To the fat remaining in the dish, add the onion, carrots and garlic, stir well and cook 2 minutes at HIGH. Place the roast over the mixture, fat side on top. Heat the brandy 1 minute at HIGH. Ignite and pour flaming over the roast. Heat the wine 40 seconds at HIGH with the remaining ingredients in a measure cup. Pour around the roast. Cover. Cook 15 minutes per pound (500 g) at MEDIUM. Check doneness, and if necessary add 15 minutes cooking.

Remove roast from dish. Stir the juice, crushing the vegetables and serve as is in a sauceboat, or cream in a food processor.

Cross Rib Roast Maison
Microwave Cooking

It is more economical to buy a cross rib with bones attached underneath. It may vary in weight from 4 to 5 pounds (2 to 2.5 kg). To make the most of such a cut, proceed as follows: remove strings, the bones will be free as they are cut by the butcher. I cook them as short beef ribs, barbecued. From the meat, I cut a thick slice of approximately 1 pound (500 g), which I put through the meat grinder to make meatballs, or I cut 4 thin slices which I tenderize using a meat mallet, for minute steaks. I braise the remaining piece as in the following recipe. Buying the ground beef, minute steaks and cross rib roast separately would cost you more.

Here is how to cook your cross rib roast:

A 3 to 4-lb (1.5 to 2 kg) cross rib roast	2 onions, thinly sliced
2 tbsp. (30 mL) margarine	2 garlic cloves, minced
1 tsp. (5 mL) salt	1/4 cup (60 mL) chili sauce
1/2 tsp. (2 mL) pepper	1 cup (250 mL) hot tea
1 small unpeeled lemon, thinly sliced	1/2 tsp. (2 mL) basil
2 tsp. (10 mL) sugar	1 tsp. (5 mL) savory

Place the meat in a 8-cup (2 L) ceramic or glass baking dish. Mix together the margarine, salt, pepper and sugar. Spread the raw part of the meat with the mixture. Cover whole with lemon slices.

Mix the remaining ingredients together and pour over the meat. Cover tightly with the dish lid or plastic wrap. Cook 20 minutes at HIGH. Turn the meat, cover and cook 30 minutes at MEDIUM. Turn and baste meat with the juice accumulated in the dish. Cover and cook 20 minutes at MEDIUM. Check doneness with a fork. If the roast is tender, cover and let stand 20 minutes before serving. It will remain warm.

Serve with noodles or rice or mashed potatoes and a bowl of grated cheese.

Braised Cross Rib Roast, Bavarian Style
Microwave Cooking

The onions browned in butter and the fresh tomatoes will give a smooth pink gravy. As for any braised meat, the cooking period is slower and longer than for roasting. Serve with parsleyed noodles and green peas.

3 tbsp. (50 mL) butter or margarine

2 medium onions, thinly sliced

A 3 to 4-lb (1.5 to 2 kg) cross rib roast

1½ tsp. (7 mL) salt

1/2 tsp. (2 mL) pepper

1/2 tsp. (2 mL) sugar

1/2 cup (125 mL) fresh tomatoes, sliced

2 tbsp. (30 mL) flour

1/2 cup (125 mL) wine or white vermouth

1/2 cup (125 mL) sour cream
  (commercial type)

Melt the butter in an 8 x 12-inch (20 x 30 cm) glass or ceramic baking dish, 3 minutes at HIGH or until browned. Add the onions, stir and cook 2 to 3 minutes at HIGH or until the onions brown here and there. Place the meat over the onions, cook 1 minute at HIGH, turn the meat and cook 4 minutes at HIGH. Add the salt, pepper and sugar. Mix together and add the tomatoes, stir well around the meat. Cover with a Pyrex lid or plastic wrap tightly fitted on the dish. Cook 15 minutes per pound (500 g) at MEDIUM.
Turn the roast, stir the sauce in the bottom of the dish and let stand, covered, 20 minutes. Place the meat on a warm platter, add the flour to the sauce, mix well. Add the wine or vermouth and the sour cream. Mix well together and cook 1 to 2 minutes at MEDIUM, or until the sauce boils lightly. Stir well and pour over the meat.

Broiled Steak, Madeira Sauce *(photo opposite page 17 top)*
Microwave Cooking

To cook a good steak in the microwave oven with a grilled meat flavor, it is important to have a ceramic browning dish (Corning). A boneless 1 or 2-inch (2.5 - 5 cm) steak is always perfect. The best cuts are the rib, spencer, club, tenderloin, strip loin, or the sirloin steak for a large steak. Have steak at room temperature, when possible.

A steak of your choice

a few pieces of fat

paprika

salt and pepper

Remove a few pieces of fat from the steak. Sprinkle one side with paprika. Preheat an 8 x 8-inch (20 x 20 cm) (Corning) 7 minutes at HIGH. Place steak in dish, without removing from oven, paprika side down. Press top of steak with finger tips for perfect contact with the dish. Put the little pieces of fat around the steak. Broil at HIGH 3 to 4 minutes depending on how you wish to have it cooked. Turn the steak, cover with waxed paper, and let it stand same time as cooking time. Steak cooks on one side only. Set on warm plate.
To make the gravy, refer to the Sauce chapter.
Pour hot sauce over the steak. Salt and pepper to taste.

Boiled Beef with Plum Sauce

Microwave Cooking

At the end of the summer, when the small blue Damson plums are sold at the market, I hasten to make this dish, which I serve with fine parsleyed noodles. Equally good hot or cold.

3 lb (1.5 kg) stewing beef	1 tsp. (5 mL) thyme
2 cups (500 mL) hot water	3 bay leaves
1-lb (500 g) marrow bone	8 to 10 sprigs of parsley (optional)
6 carrots, peeled and cut in four	1 large white onion, chopped
4 small white turnips, peeled and sliced	2 tbsp. (30 mL) butter
3 medium onions, each studded with 2 cloves	1 lb (500 g) blue plums, pitted
3 leeks, cut in 1-inch (2.5 cm) pieces	1 cup (250 mL) red wine
12 peppercorns	1 tbsp. (15 mL) sugar
1 tbsp. (15 mL) coarse salt	1/4 tsp. (1 mL) pepper

Place the meat and the marrow bone in a 12-cup (3 L) baking dish. Add the hot water. Cover, bring to the boil 15 minutes at HIGH. Add the carrots, turnips, onions, leeks, peppercorns, coarse salt, thyme, bay leaves and parsley. Stir well around the meat. Cover and cook at MEDIUM-HIGH 1 hour, stir and cook 45 minutes at MEDIUM. According to the meat cut, cooking may require 20 minutes more or less. It is good to check with a fork after 25 minutes of cooking at MEDIUM.

Melt the butter 2 minutes at HIGH in a 4-cup (1 L) dish. Add chopped onion and 1/3 cup (80 mL) red wine, cook 3 minutes at HIGH, stirring twice. Sprinkle with sugar and pepper, mix well. Add the plums and the remaining wine, stir well, cover and cook 8 to 10 minutes at MEDIUM-HIGH, or until the plums are tender. Stir well. Serve in thin slices with the plum sauce in a sauceboat.

Boiled Beef (p. 34) →

Oxtail Stew Fermière
Microwave Cooking

This is an economical family dish. At my table it is an unfailing success. I even serve this dish to friends, with boiled parsleyed potatoes. In summer, I replace the parsley with fresh chives. It is easily prepared a day ahead and reheats well, usually, 20 minutes at MEDIUM, covered.

1 oxtail, cut in small pieces	1 tsp. (2 mL) coarse or fine salt
1 small yellow turnip, peeled and cut in four	1/2 tsp. (2 mL) black peppercorns
4 medium onions, whole and peeled	2 cups (500 mL) hot water or tomato juice
2 medium carrots, whole and peeled	3 tbsp. (50 mL) flour
1 tsp. (5 mL) thyme	1/2 cup (125 mL) cold water
1/2 tsp. (2 mL) dry mustard	

Place all the ingredients, except the flour and cold water, in a 6-cup (1.5 L) ceramic, glass or plastic dish with a good cover. Cover and cook 2 minutes at HIGH, stir well and cook 40 to 60 minutes at MEDIUM, stirring 3 times, and checking the meat for doneness. When tender, stop cooking.
Mix together the flour and cold water. Remove meat from bones, cut the carrots in 3 pieces. Add the flour mixture. Stir well, cover and cook at HIGH 2 to 3 minutes, or until the sauce is creamy; stir once during cooking. Place the meat in the sauce and heat 1 minute, if necessary.

My Grandmother's "Pot en Pot"
Microwave Cooking

This is my favorite braised roast. I tried it one day in the microwave oven, adapting it, of course. My grandmother made it in an earthenware pot which I have replaced with my blue and white ceramic casserole (Panasonic). And to my surprise, the roast was even tastier than by the old-fashioned method.

3 to 4 lb (1.5 to 2 kg) beef round from sirloin tip round bone	2 large onions, thinly sliced
2 tbsp. (30 mL) soft butter	1 cup (250 mL) chili sauce
1/4 tsp. (1 mL) fresh ground pepper	1 tsp. (5 mL) basil or savory
1 large unpeeled lemon, diced	1/4 cup (60 mL) red wine or water

Set the meat in the baking dish. Spread the soft butter on top, salt and pepper. Mix together the lemon and onions and place on top of the meat. Mix the remaining ingredients together and pour over all. Cover and cook at MEDIUM 1 hour 30 minutes, or until the meat is tender. To serve, slice thinly and cover with the well-stirred or strained gravy. Accompany with potatoes and carrots mashed together, for which you will find a recipe in the Vegetable Book.

← Top: Chinese Green Pepper Steak (p. 35)
← Bottom left: Hamburger (p. 36)
← Bottom right: Small Ground Beef Timbale (p. 36)

Boiled Beef *(photo opposite page 32)*
Microwave Cooking

An old Quebec recipe, a spring dish par excellence, light and colorful. The parsleyed French dressing adds greenness. Delicious hot, it loses none of its flavor served cold, thinly sliced. One thing to remember, the meat must cool, refrigerated, in its stock, but it should stand at room temperature one hour before serving. Dice the remaining vegetables and add to leftover stock, with rice to taste, and you will have a delicious vegetable soup.

8 cups (2 L) hot water	2 bay leaves
4 to 6 medium carrots, peeled and cut in two	1 tsp. (5 mL) coarse salt
2 to 3 parsnips, peeled and cut in two	1/4 tsp. (1 mL) fresh ground pepper
1 large onion, cut in four	4 lb (2 kg) stewing beef of your choice
1/2 tsp. (2 mL) thyme	1 lb (500 g) fresh beans or green peas
4 cloves	6 to 8 potatoes, peeled

Place all the ingredients in a 10 to 12-cup (2.5 to 3 L) dish with a good cover. Cover and cook 20 minutes at HIGH. Stir, turn the meat, cover and cook 20 minutes at HIGH. Turn the meat and simmer 30 minutes at MEDIUM. Turn the meat once again and cook 20 to 30 minutes at MEDIUM, or until the meat is tender.

Parsleyed French Dressing
Place in a bowl 1/2 tsp. (2 mL) salt, 1/4 tsp. (1 mL) each of pepper and sugar, 1 tsp. (5 mL) Dijon mustard, 3 tbsp. (50 mL) wine or cider vinegar. Stir well together and add 1/3 cup (80 mL) peanut oil. Stir and add 1/4 cup (60 mL) each parsley and chives or finely chopped green onions. Mix well together, this will give a rather thick dressing. Serve in an attractive sauceboat, with each person pouring the dressing to his taste over the meat and vegetables, hot or cold.

Chinese Green Pepper Steak (photo opposite page 33 top)
Microwave Cooking

This recipe allows you to serve 4 to 5 people with one pound (500 g) of steak. I use a steak cut in one piece from a cross rib, as described for minute steaks, or 1 pound (500 g) round steak. Serve with boiled rice.

1 lb (500 g) steak in one piece or thinly sliced

3 tbsp. (50 mL) salad oil

1 garlic clove, chopped fine

1 onion, chopped

2 green peppers, slivered

1/2 tsp. (2 mL) salt

1/4 tsp. (1 mL) pepper

1 tbsp. (15 mL) fresh ginger, grated

1 tbsp. (15 mL) cornstarch

1 cup (250 mL) consommé of your choice

1 tbsp. (15 mL) soy sauce

1 tsp. (5 mL) sugar

Slice the steak on the bias as thinly as possible. Heat the oil in a browning dish (Corning) 2 minutes at HIGH. Add the garlic and heat 40 seconds at HIGH. Add the meat, stir well in the hot oil. Cook 2 minutes at HIGH. Place the meat around the dish. Set the onion, green pepper, salt, pepper and the ginger in the center, stir the whole without disturbing the meat. Cover with a waxed paper and cook 5 minutes at MEDIUM-HIGH.

Mix together the cornstarch, consommé, soy sauce and sugar. Pour over all after the 5-minute cooking period. Mix together the meat and vegetables. Cook 2 to 3 minutes at MEDIUM-HIGH, stirring after 2 minutes. The dish is ready when the sauce is transparent. Stir and serve.

Small Ground Beef Timbales (photo opposite page 33 bottom right)
Microwave Cooking

A timbale is a small glass bowl (Pyrex) or earthenware or ceramic. Ground beef patties cooked in this manner are easy to prepare and elegant.

1 lb (500 g) ground beef, quite lean	**4 green onions, chopped fine**
1/2 cup (125 mL) light cream	**4 soda crackers, crushed**
1 egg, lightly beaten	**1/2 tsp. (2 mL) salt**
1/2 cup (125 mL) quick-cooking rolled oats	**1/4 tsp. (1 mL) pepper**
2 tbsp. (30 mL) celery, chopped fine	**1/2 tsp. (2 mL) thyme or tarragon**

Mix all the ingredients together in a bowl, with your finger tips. Divide evenly into 6 to 8 buttered 6-oz. (170 g) molds. Set in a circular pattern in the oven tray. Cover with waxed paper or each one with plastic wrap. Cook 5 minutes at HIGH. Let stand 5 minutes. Unmold in a hot dish or individually on warm plates and cover with a Timbale Mushroom Sauce — See Sauce chapter.

Hamburgers (photo opposite page 33 bottom left)
Microwave Cooking

Hamburgers are cooked delicious and tender in the microwave oven, if you have a browning dish (Corning). If you do not have a browning dish, cook according to the method given below.

1 lb (500 g) ground beef	**3 tbsp. (50 mL) instant potato flakes or soft breadcrumbs**
1 tsp. (5 mL) salt	**3 tbsp. (50 mL) water, wine, apple juice or beer**
1/4 tsp. (1 mL) pepper	**Paprika**
1/2 tsp. (2 mL) thyme	
3 green onions, chopped fine	

Mix all the ingredients together in a bowl, except the paprika, with the finger tips. Divide into 4 or 5 equal-size patties. Sprinkle with paprika on one side. Preheat an 8 x 8 inch (20 x 20 cm) browning dish (Corning) 7 minutes at HIGH. Without removing dish from the oven, place the patties in it paprika side down. Cook 4 minutes at HIGH. Turn the patties and let stand 4 minutes in the dish covered with waxed paper. Serve.

To cook hamburgers without a browning dish
Mix all the ingredients in the same manner. Replace paprika with Kitchen Bouquet sauce. Place the hamburgers in an 8 x 8-inch (20 x 20 cm) dish, on a microwave rack, if possible. Cook 4 minutes at HIGH, turn the patties and complete cooking 4 minutes at MEDIUM-HIGH.

To vary the flavor of hamburgers

Add one of the following to basic meat mixture or vary meats used:

Meat variations
1. Replace 1 lb (500 g) of ground beef with 1/2 lb (250 g) veal and 1/2 lb (250 g) pork.
2. Mix 1/2 lb (250 g) ground beef with an equal quantity of ground pork.
3. Mix together 1/3 lb (160 g) each of ground beef, veal and pork.

To the meat mixture of your choice or simply to ground beef, prepared following the Hamburger recipe, add one of the following ingredients to give the patties a distinct flavor:
1. 1 tbsp. (15 mL) A-1 sauce
2. 1 tbsp. (15 mL) Worcestershire sauce
3. 1 tbsp. (15 mL) toasted dried onion
4. 4 fresh green onions, both green and white parts
5. 1/2 tsp. (2 mL) garlic powder or 1 clove crushed
6. 1 tbsp. (15 mL) ketchup or chili sauce
7. 2 tsp. (10 mL) Dijon mustard
8. 1 tsp. (5 mL) curry powder
9. 1 tsp. (5 mL) ground cumin and the juice of 1 lemon
10. 2 tbsp. (30 mL) lemon juice, instead of water, 1/4 tsp. (1 mL) thyme
11. 2 tbsp. (30 mL) red wine and 1 tsp. (5 mL) oregano
12. 1 tsp. (5 mL) basil, 1 tsp. (5 mL) coriander, powder or grains, 1 garlic clove, chopped fine.

A few toppings for cooked hamburgers
1. Place a slice of cheese of your choice over each. Heat 40 seconds at HIGH.
2. Sprinkle 1/2 tsp. (2 mL) grated Parmesan cheese over each patty, heat at MEDIUM-HIGH 20 seconds.
3. Put a tsp. (5 mL) of sour cream on top of each patty, sprinkle with paprika and serve.
4. Sprinkle each one with 1 tsp. (5 mL) or 1 tbsp. (15 mL) of dry onion soup mixture. Heat 20 seconds at HIGH.
5. Place over each hamburger 1/2 tsp. (2 mL) butter mixed with 1/2 tsp. (2 mL) fresh chives.

Cottage Cheese Meat Patties
Microwave Cooking

The melted butter added to the meat places this recipe in the Gourmet roster.

1 lb (500 g) ground beef, *lean*
1/2 cup (125 mL) cottage cheese
1 egg, lightly beaten
3 tbsp. (50 mL) melted butter

1 tsp. (5 mL) salt
3 green onions, chopped fine
1/2 tsp. (2 mL) thyme

Mix all the ingredients together without crushing the meat too much. Form into 4 large or 6 medium patties.
Preheat a browning dish (Corning) 4 minutes.
Sprinkle paprika over the patties. Set them in the hot dish without removing it from the oven. Press each patty down for a good contact. Cook 6 minutes at HIGH, turn the patties and let stand (without cooking) 5 minutes in the oven. The internal heat in the patties will finish cooking. Serve.

Bacon Meat Roll
Microwave Cooking

A delicious meat loaf, the best, to my knowledge. It is equally good hot or cold and it cooks to perfection in the microwave oven.

1 lb (500 g) ground beef of your choice
1 cup (125 mL) soda crackers, crushed
1 medium onion, minced
2 beaten eggs
1/4 cup (60 mL) light or rich cream

1 tsp. (5 mL) salt
1/4 tsp. (1 mL) each pepper and nutmeg
1/2 tsp. (2 mL) each thyme and allspice
6 to 8 slices bacon

Place all the ingredients, except the bacon, in a bowl. Mix well and form into a roll.
Set the slices of bacon side by side on a sheet of waxed paper. Place the meat in the middle of the bacon. Using the waxed paper bring the ends of the bacon slices on to the meat. Repeat the process on the other side. Form into one large roll, which is easy if you roll it slightly on the table tightening it with the waxed paper.
Place the roll in an 8 x 8-inch (20 x 20 cm) dish, cook at HIGH 11 to 12 minutes, until the bacon on top is well browned. Remove from dish with a wide spatula. Serve hot or cold.

Homemade Meat Loaf
Microwave Cooking

This meat loaf, prepared in a jiffy, well flavored, good hot or cold, can be kept one week, well covered, in the refrigerator. It also lends itself well for delicious sandwiches with a few leaves of lettuce and a bit of celery.

1/3 cup (80 mL) fine breadcrumbs

1 cup (250 mL) milk

1½ lb (750 g) ground beef

2 eggs, well beaten

1 tsp. (5 mL) salt

1/4 tsp. (1 mL) pepper

1 tsp. (5 mL) sage or savory

Topping:

1 tbsp. (15 mL) brown sugar

1/4 cup (60 mL) ketchup

1/4 tsp. (1 mL) nutmeg

1 tsp. (5 mL) dry mustard

Mix together in a Pyrex or ceramic loaf pan the first 7 ingredients. Mix the topping ingredients, spread on top of the meat. Cover with waxed paper. Cook 20 minutes at MEDIUM-HIGH. Serve hot or cold.

Monique's Meat Loaf *(first photo back top)*
Microwave Cooking

This quickly prepared meat loaf was one of my daughter Monique's favorite recipes. She served it surrounded with elbow macaroni mixed with butter, fresh parsley and chives.

2 lb (1 kg) ground beef or a mixture of pork,
   veal and beef

One 10-oz. (284 mL) can vegetable soup

1 egg

1/2 tsp. (2 mL) salt

1/4 tsp. (1 mL) pepper

1/2 tsp. (2 mL) garlic powder

2 tbsp. (30 mL) cheddar cheese, grated

Place all the ingredients in a bowl and mix. Pour into a 9 x 5-inch (22.5 x 12.5 cm) loaf pan. Cover with plastic wrap. Cook 20 minutes at MEDIUM-HIGH. Serve hot or cold. I prefer to eat it cold.

Short Beef Ribs, Barbecued *(photo opposite page 97 bottom)*
Microwave Cooking

Here is a way to cook the beef ribs removed from the cross rib. They can also be bought separately. Spareribs may also be prepared in the same manner. Serve with plain rice; for a more elaborate meal, garnish with broiled mushrooms.

2 to 3 lb (1 to 1.5 kg) short beef ribs	20 peppercorns
1/2 cup (125 mL) ketchup or chili sauce	1 tsp. (5 mL) savory
1 cup (250 mL) water	4 garlic cloves, cut in two
1 tbsp. (15 mL) sugar	2 large onions, sliced thick
1 tbsp. (15 mL) prepared mustard	juice and grated rind of one orange
1 tsp. (5 mL) salt	3 tbsp. (50 mL) soy sauce

Place the beef ribs in a bowl. Mix the remaining ingredients. Pour over the beef ribs and mix thoroughly, cover and refrigerate 24 hours, stirring 2 to 3 times during the marinating period. To cook, place the meat and marinade in an 8 to 10-cup (4 to 5 L) baking dish. Cover, cook at HIGH 20 minutes, stir well and cook at MEDIUM 30 to 40 minutes, or until the meat is tender. Stir twice during the cooking period at MEDIUM.

Florentine Meat Loaf
Microwave Cooking

Veal often replaces beef, as it is easier to buy veal in Florence. Both meats give excellent results.

1½ lb (750 g) ground beef	1/2 cup (125 mL) fresh tomatoes, unpeeled, diced
1 egg	
1/2 cup (125 mL) fine breadcrumbs	1 tbsp. (15 mL) brown sugar
1/2 cup (125 mL) fresh mushrooms, thinly sliced	2 tbsp. (30 mL) cream or milk
	grated rind of 1 lemon
1 tbsp. (15 mL) rolled oats	1 tsp. (5 mL) basil
1 onion, chopped fine	1/2 tsp. (2 mL) each salt and pepper

Mix all the ingredients together in a bowl. Place in a glass loaf pan. Sprinkle generously with paprika. Cook 20 minutes at MEDIUM-HIGH. Let stand 10 minutes before serving.

Genoese Beef Casserole
Microwave Cooking

I often make this casserole when I remove 1 pound (500 g) of beef for grinding from a piece of meat. It is important to use fine noodles.

1 lb (500 g) ground beef

1½ cups (375 mL) fine noodles, in 1-inch (2.5 cm) pieces

1 onion, chopped fine

1 cup (250 mL) celery, diced

2 cups (500 mL) tomato juice

1 tsp. (5 mL) sugar

1 tsp. (5 mL) savory or thyme

1/2 tsp. (2 mL) each of salt and pepper

Set the ground beef in a 4-cup (1 L) baking dish, sprinkle the noodles, onion and celery over the meat. Mix together the tomato juice and remaining ingredients and pour over the meat.
Cover and cook 10 minutes at high. Mix well and cook 10 minutes more at MEDIUM. Stir, cover and let stand 10 minutes. Serve with a bowl of grated cheese.

Veal

Veal

Chefs often refer to veal as the "Chameleon" of cooking. It is a meat which has an affinity with all flavors: thyme, tarragon, rosemary, sage, orange and lemon, tomato and white wine, to name but a few. The Italians are the greatest veal eaters.

There are two kinds of veal, the milk-fed veal and the grass-fed veal. The milk-fed is the very best. The milk-fed calf was fed its mother's milk, the meat is pinkish-white, the fat, ivory-white color. It is becoming more and more difficult to come by and its cost is high.

The grass-fed calf is fed powdered milk and let out in the pasture. Its meat is redder, it is also firmer, and it does cost less.

What you should know about Veal

- Avoid freezing veal, especially milk-fed veal, as it loses much of its flavor and moisture.
- Ground veal and scallops should be cooked no more than two days after buying.
- As for other meats, veal should be at room temperature before roasting in the microwave oven.
- For a perfect roast in the microwave oven, veal must not be overcooked. It must not roast as brown as lamb or beef, which dries it up. It should be lightly browned and basted 2 or 3 times during the cooking period.
- It is important to place veal scallops between two sheets of waxed paper before pounding with a meat mallet, so as to prevent moisture from escaping from the meat.
- Veal chops will be more tender and well browned when coated with a mixture of flour, paprika and an aromatic herb of your choice, and then browned in very hot oil, in preference to butter, especially if olive oil is used. For this procedure, a microwave browning dish must be used.
- Veal is well done when it registers 170°F (96°C) on the meat thermometer.
- To obtain a perfect roast of veal cooked in the microwave oven, choose a 3-lb (1.5 kg) roast.
- Garlic, tarragon and thyme are the perfect flavorings for a roast of veal. Madeira sauce, all mushroom and tomato sauces are very good with veal (See Sauce Chapter).

Veal Cuts

Loin roast — is divided into two parts: the rib roast and the loin roast.

The loin roast, is the meaty end of the whole loin which contains the T-shape bones and the tenderloin. Its price is quite high as it is usually sold sliced into chops, which are the loin chops. It contains the tenderloin. A very good piece of meat roasted in the microwave oven. But it must be boned and rolled.

The rib roast, the less meaty part of the whole loin, contains rib bones and no tenderloin. It is a little less expensive. It is better to have it deboned and rolled. That is my favorite cut for braising.

Shoulder roast, is sold boned and rolled or cut into shoulder chops. It is used for simmered steaks or cubed for stewing; rolled and tied, it is braised or roasted by convection.

The upper and lower parts of the leg or veal round — the upper end is more tender. It may be roasted or braised. The lower part makes a good simmered roast.

- Veal steaks or veal scallops are excellent taken from the mid-section of the leg.

Rib chops, are cut triangular in shape and contain the rib bones.

Veal shank, is one of my favorite cuts for braising. It may be used for stewing, or simmered at MEDIUM or with the "Sensor".

The breast, is the cut next to the round shoulder. Boned and ground, I consider it to be the best for ground veal.

Leg of Veal Roast "à la Française"
Convection Cooking

The upper part of the leg is more tender than the lower, but this upper part is more difficult to carve. In roasting veal, there are two important factors to remember, its fat content is lower and it has a higher proportion of muscular tissue. Therefore, slow cooking is recommended for a veal roast. Well done, it will be brownish-red outside and greyish-white inside, and the internal juice will flow easily into the serving plate.

A 4 to 5-lb (2 to 2.5 kg) leg of veal	2 tbsp. (30 mL) butter
2 - 3 garlic cloves, peeled and cut in two	3 tbsp. (50 mL) margarine
1 tsp. (5 mL) salt	Grated rind of half a lemon
1/2 tsp. (2 mL) pepper	2 tsp. (10 mL) dry mustard
1 tsp. (5 mL) thyme or tarragon	1 - 2 onions, peeled and thinly sliced

Make slits in the meat and fill with garlic halves. Mix the remaining ingredients except the onions. Place the roast on the low rack and spread the mixture all over the meat. Preheat oven to 350°F (180°C) before placing the meat in it.
Place the spatter shield in the oven ceramic tray, and place a pie plate in it, then the rack with the meat (See your oven operation manual on Convection Cooking). Cook 25 minutes per pound. Baste twice during cooking with the juices accumulated in the plate, or with 1/4 cup (60 mL) brandy.

Variation: Peel 6 medium potatoes and 6 medium onions. Spread Kitchen Bouquet over each, and place around the roast on the rack as you set the roast on it. The whole meal cooks to perfection all at once.

Slovina Veal Roast
With Temperature Probe or Comb

A Polish method of cooking a roast of veal. The vegetables with the meat juices make a creamy gravy. Whatever the instructions on your oven, I cook this roast following instructions given for Beef Medium; usually, veal is not indicated even though it does cook very well in the microwave oven, no matter what method is used.

4 bacon slices, cut into sticks	1/2 cup (125 mL) grated carrots
A 3 to 4-lb (1.5 to 2 kg) loin or leg roast, boned and rolled	1/4 cup (60 mL) thinly sliced celery
1 tsp. (5 mL) salt	1/4 cup (60 mL) table cream
1/2 tsp. (2 mL) pepper	2 tsp. (10 mL) flour
1 tsp. (5 mL) marjoram or savory	1/2 cup (125 mL) beef broth or white wine
1/4 tsp. (1 mL) thyme	1/2 lb (250 g) mushrooms, thinly sliced
3 tbsp. (50 mL) soft butter	3 tbsp. (50 mL) minced parsley
1 cup (250 mL) onions, diced	

Place the bacon pieces in a small dish, cover with hot water. Cook 3 minutes at HIGH. Drain.

Make 6 to 8 slits in the meat with the point of a knife, and fill each one with a little bacon.

Mix together the salt, pepper, marjoram or savory and the thyme with the creamed butter; put a little in each slit and spread the remaining mixture over the roast. Place the meat in an 8 x 13-inch (20 x 32.5 cm) glass dish, and stir the vegetables and cream around it.

Insert the temperature probe into the side of the meat, plug into the oven, place on the low rack in the oven, program at "Comb or Probe" at BEEF MEDIUM RARE. Start the oven; the probe will decide on the cooking time and will stop cooking automatically.

When the roast is cooked, remove the probe with oven mitts, as it is hot, and place the roast on a plate. Keep warm.

Pour the juice and vegetables from the baking dish into a food processor or a blender. Cream.

Mix the flour with the residue in the baking dish. Add the beef broth or the white wine; mix together; add the sliced mushrooms and the minced parsley. Stir well and cook 4 minutes at HIGH, stirring halfway through cooking. Add the creamed vegetables, mix together and cook 3 minutes at HIGH. Serve separately in a sauceboat or pour around the meat.

Rosemary Veal Roast *(photo opposite page 48)*
Microwave Cooking

A tender and juicy roast, light-pink in the center, as it should be. For a variation, a mushroom sauce may be added to the meat juices just before serving (See Sauce Chapter).

Basting Sauce:

1 tbsp. (15 mL) olive oil or melted butter	1/2 tsp. (2 mL) salt
1 tsp. (5 mL) paprika	1 garlic clove, chopped fine
1 tsp. (5 mL) Kitchen Bouquet sauce	1 tsp. (5 mL) rosemary
1/2 tsp. (2 mL) brown sugar	A 3 to 4-lb (1.5 to 2 kg) rib or shoulder
1/4 tsp. (1 mL) pepper	roast, boned and rolled

Mix the olive oil or melted butter with the paprika, Kitchen Bouquet and brown sugar.

Crush together in a plate the salt, pepper, garlic and rosemary. Make incisions in the meat here and there with the point of a knife. Stuff each one with the mixture. Baste the roast with the oil mixture.

Place the roast, preferably in an 8 x 8-in. (20 x 20 cm) ceramic or Pyrex baking dish. Cover with waxed paper. Cook 15 minutes at HIGH, turn the roast and baste with the pan juices. Then cook 10 minutes per pound (not counting first 15 minutes at MEDIUM-HIGH). Turn the roast once again halfway through the cooking at MEDIUM-HIGH; baste all over and continue cooking.

When cooked, place the roast on a warm platter, cover with aluminum foil and let stand in a warm place for 20 minutes. If you have a meat thermometer, insert it through the foil. It should register between 160°F and 170°F (82°C and 87°C) after a few minutes.

To make gravy with the cooking juices, simply add 1/2 cup (125 mL) of a liquid of your choice: Port, Madeira, chicken broth, cold tea or red wine. Stir and heat 2 minutes at HIGH.

Lemon Braised Veal

Microwave Cooking

For me, this braised veal is "Paris in the Spring". It is easy to prepare. I adapted it to the microwave oven a long time ago. In Paris, it is served with cubed potatoes browned in butter, then mixed with lots of parsley and chives, chopped fine, and a plain watercress salad.

2 tbsp. (30 mL) olive or vegetable oil

A 3 lb (1.5 kg) veal shoulder, rolled

Paprika

1 tsp. (5 mL) salt

1/4 tsp. (1 mL) mace

1/2 tsp. (2 mL) pepper, fresh ground

1/2 tsp. (2 mL) tarragon

1 unpeeled lemon, thinly sliced

1 large tomato, diced small

1/2 tsp. (2 mL) sugar

Heat a browning dish 7 minutes at HIGH, pour oil into it and heat 2 minutes at HIGH. Pat the meat dry with absorbent paper. Place it in the hot oil, without removing dish from oven, fat side down. Brown 5 minutes at HIGH. Remove roast from dish, place in an 8 x 13-inch (20 x 32.5 cm) glass dish, the browned fat side on top. Sprinkle with paprika, salt, pepper, mace and tarragon. Top with lemon slices. Place the diced tomato around the meat, sprinkle with the sugar. Cover with plastic wrap. Cook 20 minutes at HIGH. Stir the dish to move the juices in the bottom, but do not uncover the meat. Return to the oven and cook 35 minutes at MEDIUM. Let stand 20 minutes in a warm place before serving. Remove the lemon slices. Place the juice in a bowl, add 2 tbsp. (30 mL) cream or Madeira. Mix well and heat 2 minutes at HIGH.

Rosemary Veal Roast (p. 47) →

Veal Hash with Dumplings
Microwave Cooking

Dumplings cooked in the microwave are light and cook very fast. This dish is a complete meal, veal, vegetables, sauce, and the dumplings replacing potatoes.

1/3 cup (80 mL) flour	1 cup (250 mL) celery, diced
1 tsp. (5 mL) salt	6 small whole carrots
1/4 tsp. (1 mL) pepper	or
2 lb (1 kg) veal shoulder, cubed	1 cup (250 mL) carrots, thinly sliced
3 tbsp. (50 mL) vegetable oil or butter	2½ cups (625 mL) hot water or chicken broth

Dumplings:

1½ cups (375 mL) flour	1/2 tsp. (2 mL) salt
1 tsp. (5 mL) minced parsley	2/3 cup (160 mL) milk
1/2 tsp. (2 mL) savory	1 egg
2 tsp. (10 mL) baking powder	2 tbsp. (30 mL) vegetable oil

Mix together the flour, salt and pepper. Roll the veal cubes in the mixture. Heat 3 minutes at HIGH in an 8-cup (2 L) dish.

Heat the vegetable oil or the butter. Place the veal cubes in the hot oil, cook 2 minutes at HIGH, stir, cook again 2 minutes at HIGH. Add celery and carrots. Stir, add water or chicken broth. Cover and cook 40 minutes at MEDIUM, or until the meat is tender. Stir twice during cooking.

Prepare the dumplings as follows:
Mix together in a bowl the flour, parsley, savory, baking powder and salt.
Place in another bowl the milk, egg and oil. Mix the two together only when ready to add to the veal cooking juices. Remove the meat from the juices. Keep in a warm place.
Mix together the ingredients in the two bowls just enough to blend. If stirred too much the dumplings will not be as light. Drop into the broth with a tablespoon, all around the dish and in the center.
Cover and cook 6 minutes at HIGH. They are cooked when the dumplings are no longer shiny. Place around the veal and pour the sauce over all.

◄— Top left: Veal Shank "Osso Bucco" (p. 51)
◄— Top right: Calves' Brains in Browned Butter (p. 50)
◄— Bottom: Veau dans le Chaudron (p. 50)

Veau dans le Chaudron *(photo opposite page 49 bottom)*
Microwave Cooking

An old Québec recipe, which I like very much. One day I tried it in the microwave oven, wondering what it would be like. To my surprise, it was superb.

3 tbsp. (50 mL) vegetable oil or bacon fat

2 garlic cloves, cut in two

A 3 to 4-lb veal leg or shoulder, boned and rolled

1 tbsp. (15 mL) Kitchen Bouquet sauce

1 tsp. (5 mL) salt

1/4 tsp. (1 mL) pepper

1/2 tsp. (2 mL) thyme

1/4 tsp. (1 mL) savory

1 bay leaf

6 medium potatoes, peeled

6 medium onions, peeled, whole

Heat the oil or the bacon fat 5 minutes at HIGH, in an 8-cup (2 L) ceramic baking dish. Baste the meat with the Kitchen Bouquet. Place it in the hot fat. Cook 8 minutes at HIGH.

Turn the meat, sprinkle top with salt, pepper, thyme, savory and bay leaf. Place the potatoes and onions around it. Cover and cook 40 to 50 minutes at MEDIUM, or until the meat is tender. The shoulder will take a little longer to cook than the leg.

Note: There is no liquid to add to this recipe. Cooked in this way the meat has enough juice to make its own gravy. Some veal cuts release more moisture than others. Should there be too much juice after cooking, simply remove roast to a warm plate, surround with the potatoes and onions. Keep in a warm place. Return the baking dish to the microwave oven, uncovered. Boil the juice 3 to 6 minutes at HIGH or until the desired consistency is reached. Serve in a sauceboat.

Calves' Brains in Browned Butter
Microwave Cooking
(photo opposite page 49 top right)

A very easy dish to cook in the microwave oven, known as a great favorite among amateur gourmets. The only garnish required is a few pickled capers.

3 to 4 calves' brains

3 cups (750 mL) cold water

3 tbsp. (50 mL) vinegar of your choice

2 bay leaves

2 whole garlic cloves

1 tsp. (5 mL) salt

10 peppercorns

2 cups (500 mL) hot water

3 tbsp. (50 mL) butter

1 tbsp. (15 mL) minced parsley

1 tsp. (5 mL) pickled capers

Soak the calves' brains one hour in the cold water and vinegar. Drain and remove the red veins and small black spots on top of the brains (this is easy to do). Place them in a clean dish with the bay leaves, garlic, salt, peppercorns and hot water. Cover and cook 4 minutes at HIGH. Let stand in cooking water 2 minutes, drain and place on a warm dish.

Put the butter in a ceramic dish and heat at HIGH 3 to 5 minutes, or until the butter is dark brown. It is important to watch closely, as browning time may vary with different brands of butter. Add the parsley and capers. Pour very hot over the brains and serve.

Veal Scallops, Tomato Sauce
Microwave Cooking

In this recipe, I use veal scallops cut from the mid-section of the leg (See Pork Cuts), or 1-inch (2.5 cm) thick veal chops. Serve with noodles mixed with fried onions or with parsley, or serve with mashed potatoes.

1/4 cup (60 mL) vegetable oil	1/2 tsp. (2 mL) salt
1 garlic clove, chopped fine	1/4 tsp. (1 mL) pepper
4 to 6 small veal scallops or chops	1/2 tsp. (2 mL) basil
1/2 tsp. (2 mL} paprika	One 7½-oz. (213 mL) can tomato sauce
2 medium onions, thinly sliced	1/2 cup (125 mL) water or white vermouth
2 tbsp. (30 mL) flour	

Preheat a Corning browning dish 7 minutes at HIGH.
Add the oil; heat 2 minutes at HIGH.
Brush one side of the scallops or chops with the paprika. Place in the hot oil, paprika side down, without removing dish from oven. Press each piece of meat down with the fingers for good contact with the bottom of the dish. Cook 3 minutes at HIGH. Turn the meat, add the garlic and onions, cook 1 minute at HIGH. Remove the scallops or chops from the dish, and add the flour, salt, pepper, and basil to the fat, stir. Add the tomato sauce, water or white vermouth. Mix well together. Cook 4 minutes at HIGH, stir. Add the veal, browned side on top and make sure the bottom part is in the sauce. Cook 3 minutes at MEDIUM and serve.

Veal Shank "Osso Bucco" *(photo opposite page 49 top left)*
Microwave Cooking

Italian method for cooking veal shanks, full of flavor, easy, and economical to prepare. It is perfect served with a dish of parsleyed long grain rice.

5 to 6 pieces of veal shank, 2 inches (5 cm) each	1 large carrot, grated
1/2 cup (125 mL) browned flour	2 garlic cloves, chopped fine
1/3 cup (80 mL) vegetable or olive oil	1 tsp. (5 mL) oregano or basil
2 medium onions, chopped fine	1/2 cup (125 mL) white wine or vermouth
1/2 cup (125 mL) celery, diced	One 19-oz. (540 mL) can of tomatoes
1/2 cup (125 mL) sliced mushrooms, fresh or canned	Grated rind of one lemon
3 tbsp. (50 mL) minced parsley	1 cup (250 mL) chicken broth
	1/2 tsp. (2 mL) sugar

Roll each piece of shank in the browned flour.
Heat the oil in an 8-cup (2 L) ceramic dish 5 minutes at HIGH.
Place the meat pieces in it side by side, and cook uncovered 5 minutes at HIGH. Turn the meat. Add the remaining ingredients. Cover and cook 1 hour at MEDIUM, turning the meat twice during the cooking. When cooked, remove meat from dish and keep in a warm place. Continue cooking the sauce 8 to 10 minutes at HIGH or until it becomes very smooth. Coat the meat with the sauce.

Veal Printanier
Microwave Cooking

A piece of veal shoulder simmered until perfectly cooked, in a light white sauce. This is one of the Quebec roster of old-fashioned recipes.

2 tbsp. (30 mL) veal fat or butter

2-lb (1 kg) veal shoulder, cut in small pieces

1 tsp. (5 mL) paprika

3 tbsp. (50 mL) butter

3 tbsp. (50 mL) flour

3 cups (750 mL) milk

1/2 tsp. (2 mL) thyme

1 bay leaf

1/4 tsp. (1 mL) marjoram

1/2 lb (250 g) mushrooms, thinly sliced

10 to 12 small white onions, peeled, whole

2 carrots, thinly sliced

1 cup (250 mL) fresh or frozen green peas

Heat the 2 tbsp. (30 mL) fat or butter 3 minutes at HIGH, in a 6-cup (1.5 L) ceramic baking dish. The butter should brown lightly; cook one minute more if necessary. Sprinkle meat with paprika, place in the browned butter, stir and cook 5 minutes at HIGH.

Make a white sauce in a 4-cup (1 L) measure cup. Place the butter in the cup, heat 2 minutes at HIGH, add the flour and mix together. Add the milk, mix, cook 2 minutes at HIGH, stir, cook 2 minutes more at HIGH, stir, and continue in this manner until you have a light white sauce. Salt and pepper to taste and add the thyme, bay leaf and marjoram. Mix together. Pour over the meat, stir, cover and cook 8 minutes at HIGH.

Add the mushrooms, onions, carrots and green peas*. Mix well together. Cover and cook 35 to 40 minutes at MEDIUM. Serve with parsleyed rice or fine noodles and a bowl of grated cheese, where each one helps himself, to taste.

* Frozen green peas are just as good as fresh peas when cooked in this manner.

Breaded Veal Chops *(photo opposite page 96)*
Microwave Cooking

Veal chops prepared in this manner will be golden and crisp. I remove them from the refrigerator one hour before cooking. I coat them with breadcrumbs and let them stand on absorbent paper for 30 minutes. I prefer to bone the chops but they also cook very well with the bone.

4 to 6 veal loin chops, 1 inch (2.5 cm) thick	2 tbsp. (30 mL) milk
3 tbsp. (50 mL) flour	2/3 cup (160 mL) fine breadcrumbs
1 tsp. (5 mL) paprika	1/2 tsp. (2 mL) rosemary or tarragon
1 beaten egg	2 tbsp. (30 mL) butter

Mix in a plate the flour and paprika. Roll each chop in the mixture, to coat them well. Beat the egg with the milk in a large plate. Mix the rosemary or tarragon and breadcrumbs in another plate. Dip each chop in the milk mixture and roll in the breadcrumbs and herbs. Let stand one hour.
Preheat a Corning browning dish 7 minutes at HIGH. Add the butter which will brown very fast. Place one chop at a time in the dish, pressing each chop down for perfect contact with the hot butter. Do this without removing dish from oven. Cook at HIGH 3 minutes, plus 3 minutes at MEDIUM. Turn the chops and let stand 10 minutes at room temperature, without cooking. Serve with a sauce of your choice (See Sauce Chapter).

Homemade Foie Gras
Convection

This "pâté" is at its best when made with calf liver. When it is too expensive or difficult to find, use half calf liver and half lamb or beef liver. It keeps 8 to 15 days in the refrigerator, tightly covered.

1 lb (500 g) calf, beef or lamb liver or a mixture of two	1 tsp. (5 mL) pepper
	2 tsp. (10 mL) salt
1/2 lb (250 g) ground pork	1 cup (250 mL) flour
1 envelope dehydrated onion soup mix	4 to 5 bay leaves
2 eggs	4 slices of bacon (optional)
1½ cups (375 mL) table cream	

Chop the calf or beef or lamb liver and the pork very fine, in the meat grinder or 40 seconds in the food processor.
Add the remaining ingredients, except the bacon slices. Mix well until creamy. Line the bottom of a Pyrex bread pan with 2 slices of bacon. Fill with the liver mixture. Top with 2 more slices of bacon. Preheat convection oven to 350°F (180°C). Place the pan on the low rack. Cook 1 hour and 20 minutes or until the top is well browned. Cool, cover and refrigerate 24 hours before serving.

Venitian Calf Liver
Microwave Cooking

I have not yet met the person who does not like calf liver and who has refused to try this dish. It is perfect with mashed potatoes and an endive or crisp Boston lettuce salad.

1 lb (500 g) calf liver

3 tbsp. (50 mL) butter

2 cups (500 mL) thinly sliced onions

1 tsp. (5 mL) salt

1/4 tsp. (1 mL) pepper

2 tbsp. (30 mL) white wine or Madeira or lemon juice

1 tbsp. (15 mL) minced parsley

Slice the liver as thinly as possible, and then cut into strips. Preheat browning dish (Corning) 7 minutes, and melt the butter in it without removing from the oven. Add the onions, mix and cook 3 minutes at HIGH. Salt, pepper. Add the liver strips, stir, cook 2 minutes at HIGH, stir and cook another 2 minutes at HIGH. Add the white or Madeira wine or the lemon juice, together with the parsley and cook 1 minute at HIGH. Stir and serve.

Pink Veal Meat Loaf
Microwave Cooking

If your oven has the Auto Sensor system or Insta-Matic, then program your oven as indicated in your operation manual. The oven will decide on the cooking time. Following this method, it is important to cover the mold with plastic wrap.

1½ lb (750 g) ground veal

1 egg, lightly beaten

1/2 cup (125 mL) stale bread, crushed

1/3 cup (80 mL) chili sauce

1/2 cup (125 mL) onion, chopped fine

2 garlic cloves, chopped fine

1 tsp. (5 mL) thyme or tarragon

Grated rind of one lemon

1/2 tsp. (2 mL) salt

1/4 tsp. (1 mL) pepper

1/4 tsp. (1 mL) nutmeg or mace

Mix together all the ingredients, except the nutmeg or mace, in a bowl. When thoroughly mixed, pack into an 8 x 4-inch (20 x 10 cm) mold. Sprinkle top with nutmeg or mace. Cover with waxed paper. Cook 20 to 22 minutes at MEDIUM-HIGH. Let stand 10 minutes before serving, when serving hot; or cool, well covered, and refrigerate 12 hours before serving.

Lamb

Lamb

For lamb as for beef, it is important to know the cuts. It is also important to know what type of cooking applies to each individual cut of lamb for perfect results.

Color and texture are very meaningful. Young quality lamb will have firm, smooth, tender, whitish pink fat. The flesh is firm to the touch, never flabby or tough with moist and pinkish bones.

The weight of the leg is a good indication of its quality. To be "perfect", it should weigh from 4 to 5 pounds (2 to 2.5 kg). When it reaches 7 pounds (3.5 kg) it is too fat, and the meat will not be as delicately flavored or as tender.

The Cuts

The carcass is split in two equal portions through the back: the Fore Quarter which is the neck end and the Hind Quarter, the leg.

The Fore Quarter

The neck: Cut just in front of the shoulder, usually 1 inch (2.5 cm) thick. This is a tender and tasty meat for making delicious casseroles, soups, etc.

The shoulder: This is the front leg of the lamb (the leg from the back is the true leg of the lamb).
Out of the shoulder are cut steaks, the ones with the round bone and those with the long bones. The shoulder is boned and rolled to make a roast; or a boned unrolled shoulder can be marinated, for a delicious roast, or cubed for tasty stews, or put through the meat grinder, for ground lamb.

The fore shanks are the two front legs of the lamb, they are simmered or made into delicious casserole dishes.

The Hind Quarter

From the hind quarter, are cut the rack and the loin chops. They are the two cuts most in demand.

The whole loin contains the loin chops and the rib section, which in one piece consists of 12 ribs. It is a deluxe cut.

The leg may be cut in two, which gives the Hind Shank Roast, usually smaller than the top of the leg; both are very tender. The top end being more meaty, it is also more expensive.

Cooking a Leg of Lamb

Since lamb is a red meat like beef, it can be roasted and it is at its best rare or medium; well done, lamb is never as good nor as tender. For perfect roasting of lamb, check with a meat thermometer (do not leave thermometer in meat during cooking. Just check and remove).

145°F (63°C) on the thermometer indicates rare

155°F (68°C) on the thermometer indicates medium

Lamb can be roasted:

- In the microwave
- By Convection Method
- With Temperature Probe
- By Auto Sensor
- By Weight

Some microwave ovens offer many of those methods, others have only one or two.

Here again, you will realize the importance of reading the oven operation manual before use, so as to be aware of all the factors.

Meat Cuts

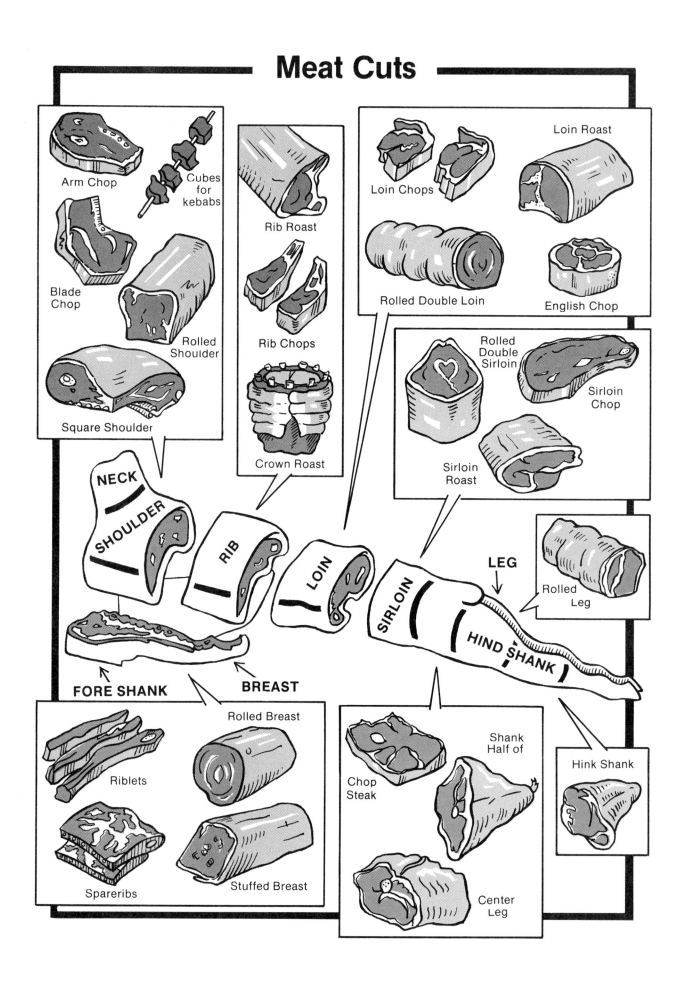

Arm Chop

Cubes for kebabs

Blade Chop

Rolled Shoulder

Square Shoulder

Rib Roast

Rib Chops

Crown Roast

Loin Chops

Loin Roast

Rolled Double Loin

English Chop

Rolled Double Sirloin

Sirloin Chop

Sirloin Roast

NECK

SHOULDER

RIB

LOIN

SIRLOIN

LEG

Rolled Leg

HIND SHANK

FORE SHANK

BREAST

Rolled Breast

Riblets

Spareribs

Stuffed Breast

Chop Steak

Shank Half of

Hink Shank

Center Leg

My Sunday Roast Leg of Lamb
Microwave Cooking

Mother often served a roast of lamb, to everyone's delight. Our favorite was the one she called "My Sunday Leg of Lamb". I have successfully adapted it to microwave cooking.

A 4 to 5-lb (2 to 2.5 kg) leg of lamb, boned and rolled

1 garlic clove, crushed

2 tsp. (10 mL) fresh grated ginger

1 tsp. (5 mL) paprika

1/4 tsp. (1 mL) pepper

1 tbsp. (15 mL) vegetable oil

Juice and rind of 1 lemon

1/2 cup (125 mL) fine breadcrumbs

Place meat on a platter. Make a clear paste with the remaining ingredients, except the breadcrumbs. Spread over the leg of lamb. Cover with waxed paper, and marinate 4 to 5 hours at room temperature. To roast the leg of lamb, when marinating time is over, place the meat on a microwave rack, in a glass 12 x 8-inch (30 x 20 cm) baking dish. Sprinkle fat top of roast with the breadcrumbs. Then pour the remaining marinating mixture into the baking dish. Cover bone tips with a strip of aluminum foil to prevent drying of the meat around the bones during cooking.
Roast 10 minutes at HIGH, lower heat to MEDIUM and roast 8 to 10 minutes, depending on whether you wish to have your roast rare or medium.
When cooked, place the roast on a warm platter. Cover and let stand 15 minutes.
In the interval, make the gravy by adding to the juice in the baking dish 1/2 cup (125 mL) cold coffee or red wine or 1/4 cup (60 mL) Madeira or "White Brandy". Stir well. Heat 3 minutes at HIGH. Pour into a sauceboat.

Rosemary Roast of Lamb
Convection

Rosemary and basil are without doubt the best flavoring herbs for roasted lamb. In Italy, the combination of rosemary and garlic is used.

A 4 to 5-lb (2 to 2.5 kg) leg of lamb

1 tsp. (5 mL) freshly ground pepper

1 tsp. (5 mL) freshly grated ginger

2 tsp. (10 mL) rosemary

1 tsp. (5 mL) basil

1 tbsp. (15 mL) vegetable oil

1/4 cup (60 mL) fine breadcrumbs

Preheat the convection section of your microwave oven at 375°F (190°C) (check for procedure in your oven operation manual).
Place the spatter shield in the oven tray, put the low rack in it with a pie plate underneath. Mix all the ingredients together and spread on top of the roast, set it on the rack. Program your oven at 375°F (190°C). Roast 15 minutes per pound. Let stand 15 minutes in a warm place before serving.
Add to the juice in the plate, 1/3 cup (80 mL) red wine or chicken broth. Scrape the bottom of the plate and crush all the browned bits. Heat 1 minute at HIGH. Pour into a sauceboat.

English Glazed Roast of Lamb *(photo opposite page 64)*
Probe or Comb

The boned and rolled shoulder may be prepared and cooked the same way as the leg. When using the Temperature Probe, all you have to do is prepare the meat, insert the probe in the meat and plug it into the oven, select the desired degree of cooking, i.e. MEDIUM-RARE for the leg, and MEDIUM for the shoulder. The oven decides on the cooking time and will automatically stop cooking when roast is cooked according to setting.

Half a leg of lamb or a whole leg of lamb	**Juice of 1 lemon**
or	**1/4 cup (60 mL) soft butter**
A boned and rolled shoulder	**1/4 cup (60 mL) fresh mint, chopped fine**
Grated rind of 1 orange	**1 tsp. (5 mL) paprika**
Juice of 2 oranges	**1/4 tsp. (1 mL) pepper**

Place the meat in a 9 x 13-inch (22.5 x 32.5 cm) glass dish. Mix the remaining ingredients. Spread over the meat. Wrap the tip of the leg with a strip of aluminum foil. Insert the temperature probe into the side of the roast (read instructions given in your oven operation manual), plug opposite end into the oven. Select desired cooking. Baste meat twice during cooking.

Note: Place the ready-to-cook roast on the low rack included with your oven accessories.

- To make the gravy, remove cooked roast to a warm platter. Add to the juice in the baking dish 1/3 cup (80 mL) cold tea. Stir well to crush the brown caramelized bits in the bottom of the dish, which gives color and flavor to the gravy. Heat 2 minutes at HIGH.

Lamb Chops Maison *(photo opposite page 81 bottom)*
Microwave Cooking

With a browning dish, you can cook lovely golden chops in the microwave oven. To my taste, they are perfect and easier to digest because of the fat which may be eliminated.

4 lamb chops	**1/2 tsp. (2 mL) rosemary or basil**
1/2 tsp. (2 mL) sugar	**1 tbsp. (15 mL) of fat removed from chops**
1/2 tsp. (2 mL) paprika	

Preheat browning dish 7 minutes at HIGH.
Mix together the sugar, paprika, rosemary or basil. Rub each chop with the mixture.
Place the pieces of fat in the browning dish without removing it from the oven. Spread in the dish with a fork and place in the center. Set each chop in the dish, pressing it down with the finger tips. Brown 6 minutes at HIGH. Turn the chops and let stand 10 minutes in the dish without cooking (internal heat will finish the cooking). Serve.

West Indian Lamb Shoulder
Microwave or Convection

This is one of my family's favorite meals, which I serve with curried fried rice and parsleyed cauliflower.

**A 3-lb (1.5 kg) lamb shoulder,
   boned and rolled**

4 garlic cloves, finely chopped

1/2 cup (125 mL) boiling water

1/3 cup (80 mL) honey

1/2 cup (125 mL) soy sauce*

The juice of 1 orange

Mix together in a large bowl the garlic, boiling water, honey and soy sauce. Roll the meat in the mixture, cover and refrigerate 24 hours before cooking.

Remove meat from marinade. Place in an 8 x 13-inch (20 x 32.5 cm) glass dish. Add 1/2 cup (125 mL) of the marinade. Cook according to one of the two following methods:

Convection: Set the low rack as indicated in your oven operation manual. Roast 25 minutes per pound in a preheated 350°F (180°C) oven.

Or

Microwave: Place the meat in the same dish with half a cup (125 mL) of the marinade. Cover with plastic wrap. Cook 15 minutes at HIGH. Turn the roast and baste with the juices. Cover and cook 15 minutes per pound (500 g) at MEDIUM.

Let stand 15 minutes before serving.

How to make the gravy:

Whether the shoulder of lamb is cooked by convection or microwave, the gravy is prepared in the same manner.

After removing the roast from the dish, add the orange juice to the liquid in the dish. To taste, 1/3 cup (80 mL) Sake (Japanese wine) may be added. Stir well. Heat 2 minutes at HIGH when ready to serve. Pour into a sauceboat.

* Japanese soy sauce is more delicate in flavour than the Chinese sauce, but either one may be used.

Portuguese Leg of Lamb with Madeira
Microwave Cooking

The combination of Madeira, garlic and lemon rind gives this roast a very distinct flavor. Serve with long grain rice boiled with grated carrots, green peas and diced green onions.

1/4 cup (60 mL) Madeira or dry sherry

1 tbsp. (15 mL) paprika

2 tbsp. (30 mL) Kitchen Bouquet sauce

2 tbsp. (30 mL) vegetable oil

2 garlic cloves, minced

Rind of 1 lemon

A 3 to 4-lb (1.5 to 2 kg) leg of lamb, boned and rolled

or

A 3 to 4-lb (1.5 to 2 kg) lamb shoulder, rolled

Mix together the first 6 ingredients in a measuring cup. Heat 2 minutes at MEDIUM-HIGH.
Place the roast on a microwave rack, place in a 12 x 8-inch (30 x 20 cm) glass dish. Baste the roast all over with the hot mixture. Cook 8 minutes at HIGH, baste the meat thoroughly with the juice in the bottom of the dish. Cook 10 minutes per pound (500 g) at MEDIUM-HIGH. When cooked, place on a hot platter, cover and let stand 15 minutes.
To make the gravy, add to the cooking juices 1/3 cup (80 mL) consommé or cream or coffee. Mix well. Heat 1 minute at HIGH when ready to serve.

Curried Poached Leg of Lamb
Microwave Cooking

Served hot, golden and well-flavored. Slice thinly and serve at room temperature. An excellent cold meat for a buffet, with fruit chutney of your choice and a curried rice salad.

Half a leg or a whole leg of lamb, boned and rolled

1 garlic clove, quartered

1 tbsp. (15 mL) rosemary

1 tsp. (5 mL) salt

1/2 tsp. (2 mL) pepper

1 tbsp. (15 mL) curry powder

6 medium carrots, whole

6 celery stalks, diced

8 to 10 medium potatoes

10 small white onions

1/2 cup (125 mL) water

1/2 cup (125 mL) cider or apple juice

Make 4 to 5 slits in the meat. Stuff each one with a piece of garlic and a pinch of rosemary.
Mix together the salt, pepper and curry powder. Sprinkle on top of the roast.
Place the meat in the center of a glass or ceramic dish, with a lid if possible. Place the vegetables around the meat. Pour the water and the cider or apple juice over the vegetables. Cover with waxed paper or plastic wrap or the lid from the dish. Cook 20 minutes at HIGH, turn the meat. Cover and cook 10 minutes per pound at MEDIUM. Let stand 15 minutes before removing lid. Place the vegetables around the roast and the gravy in a sauceboat.

Fore Shanks with Beer *(photo opposite page 81 top)*
Microwave Cooking

It is not easy to find small 1 to 2-lb (500 g to 1 kg) lamb shoulder shanks. Order them ahead of time from your butcher. They are economical, tender and easy to cook.

2 garlic cloves, cut in three	1 tsp. (5 mL) savory
2 to 4 shoulder shanks	1/4 cup (60 mL) beer of your choice
3 tbsp. (50 mL) bacon fat	1 tsp. (5 mL) sugar
3 tbsp. (50 mL) flour	2 bay leaves
1/2 tsp. (2 mL) salt	Juice and rind of one lemon
1/4 tsp. (1 mL) pepper	

Make slits in the meat and place a sliver of garlic into each. Mix together the flour, salt, pepper, savory. Coat the shanks thoroughly with the mixture.
Heat a browning dish (Corning) 7 minutes at HIGH. Add the bacon fat without removing the dish from the oven, place the floured shanks one next to the other in it. Brown 5 minutes at HIGH. Turn each piece of meat. Add the beer, sugar, bay leaves, juice and lemon rind. Cover and cook 10 minutes at HIGH. Remove the shanks to another dish, pour the gravy all around. Cover and cook 30 to 40 minutes at MEDIUM. Halfway through the cooking, baste the meat with the cooking juices.
It is sometimes necessary to allow an extra 10 to 12 minutes of cooking if the meat is less tender.
To serve, add 1/4 cup (60 mL) water or cold tea to the juices in the dish. Stir well and heat 2 minutes at HIGH when ready to serve.

Scottish Lamb Casserole
Microwave Cooking

This dish may be prepared with pieces of neck or leg or shoulder steak, cubed or thinly sliced.

2 tbsp. (30 mL) butter or bacon fat	One 19-oz. (540 mL) can tomatoes
2 onions, peeled and thinly sliced	2 tsp. (10 mL) sugar
2 lb (1 kg) cubed lamb of your choice	2 cups (500 mL) bread cubes
1 tsp. (5 mL) salt	1/4 tsp. (1 mL) aniseed
1/4 tsp. (1 mL) pepper	1/2 tsp. (2 mL) salt
1/4 tsp. (1 mL) allspice	1 tbsp. (15 mL) butter

Heat the butter or the bacon fat 4 minutes at HIGH.
Add the onions, stir well and cook 3 minutes at HIGH.
Stir and add the cubed lamb. Stir together. Cook 3 minutes at HIGH. Mix together the salt, pepper and allspice. Sprinkle over meat. Stir. Mix together the sugar and tomatoes. Pour over the meat.
Stir the bread cubes with the 1/2 tsp. (2 mL) salt and the aniseed. Sprinkle over the whole.
Dot with butter. Cover with lid or plastic wrap. Cook 10 minutes at HIGH. Uncover and cook at MEDIUM 20 to 25 minutes or until the meat is tender.
Check doneness with the point of a knife. Let stand 10 minutes in a warm place before serving.

Country Casserole *(first photo front)*
Microwave Cooking

A meal-in-a-dish!

1 lb (500 g) ground lamb	**4 small cooked potatoes**
1/2 tsp. (2 mL) basil	**4 small fresh tomatoes**
1/4 tsp. (1 mL) pepper	**1 cup (250 mL) corn kernels***
1/2 tsp. (2 mL) salt	**2 tbsp. (30 mL) grated cheese**
4 slices of bacon	

Mix together the lamb, basil, salt and pepper. Make into four patties. Wrap a slice of bacon around each patty, holding it with a wooden pick. Sprinkle with paprika.
Cook the potatoes 6 minutes at HIGH. Remove from oven and place on an absorbent paper.
Remove pulp from tomatoes and sprinkle inside with salt, pepper and a pinch of sugar. Divide the corn equally in each tomato.
Preheat a browning dish (Corning) 7 minutes at HIGH.
Place the meat patties in the dish, paprika side down, without removing it from the oven. Press each patty down with the finger tips for perfect contact between meat and dish. Cook 4 minutes at HIGH.
Turn the patties, place the cooked potatoes and stuffed tomatoes all around. Cover the dish with waxed paper, cook 4 to 5 minutes at MEDIUM-HIGH. Serve.

* *You may use canned well-drained corn kernels, or you may cook frozen corn before cooking the patties, approximately 1 cup (250 mL) of corn, cook covered without water, 4 minutes at HIGH. Drain and use.*

English Glazed Roast of Lamb (p. 60) →

Poached and Glazed Lamb Shoulder
Microwave Cooking

The mint or currant jelly glaze gives a special flavor to the meat. It can also be served without the glaze.

A 2 to 3-lb (1 to 1.5 kg) rolled lamb shoulder

1/4 cup (60 mL) butter or margarine

2 garlic cloves, finely chopped

1 tsp. (5 mL) thyme

1 tbsp. (15 mL) flour

1 tsp. (5 mL) salt

1/4 tsp. (1 mL) pepper

The rind of 1 lemon

1 tbsp. (15 mL) lemon juice

1/2 cup (125 mL) mint or currant jelly

Cream together the butter or margarine, garlic, thyme, flour, salt, pepper and lemon rind. Spread over the meat. Place in an 8 x 12-inch (20 x 30 cm) glass dish. Cover with waxed paper and refrigerate 4 to 5 hours.

When removing from refrigerator, let stand one hour on kitchen counter. Do not remove liquid which may have accumulated in the bottom of the dish. Cover with plastic wrap. Cook 15 minutes at HIGH, then reduce to MEDIUM and cook 50 minutes. Turn the meat and let stand 20 minutes in the juice.

To Glaze: Remove meat from baking dish. To the liquid in the dish, add the lemon juice and the mint or currant jelly. Stir well. Do not cover, cook at HIGH 2 to 4 minutes, or until the juice thickens, stirring twice during the cooking.

Pour over the meat and baste it 7 or 8 times. If necessary, heat roast 3 minutes at MEDIUM. Serve hot with boiled rice garnished with green peas.

Lamb Meat Balls *(photo opposite bottom)*
Microwave Cooking

Make small meat balls to serve hot as appetizers, or divide into four portions and serve as lamb patties.

1 lb (500 g) ground lamb

1/4 cup (60 mL) soy sauce*

1 garlic clove, chopped fine

1 tbsp. (15 mL) vegetable oil

1/3 cup (80 mL) plum sauce, oriental

Mix together in a bowl, the ground lamb, soy sauce and garlic. Make into small meat balls or four patties, depending on how you wish to serve them.

Heat the vegetable oil 3 minutes at HIGH, in a ceramic dish. Sprinkle the meat balls or the patties with paprika. Pour them into or place them in the hot oil. Cook the meat balls 5 minutes at HIGH, stirring twice. Cook the patties 3 minutes at HIGH, turn and cook 2 minutes at HIGH.

Add the plum sauce to the meat balls, shake the dish to coat them with the sauce. Heat 2 minutes at HIGH, stir and serve.

For the patties, baste the top of each with the plum sauce, baste with some of the juice accumulated in the bottom of the dish. Cover with waxed paper and cook 3 minutes at HIGH. Serve.

* Japanese soy sauce is more delicate in flavor than the Chinese sauce, but either one may be used.

← Top: Baked Lamb Liver (p. 66)
← Bottom: Lamb Meat Balls (p. 65)

Baked Lamb Liver *(photo opposite page 65 top)*

Convection

A whole 1 or 2-lb (500 g or 1 kg) lamb liver roasted in one piece is excellent served hot or cold. Slice it thinly and serve it hot with its sauce; cold, with a cranberry sauce, or hot with chutney to taste.

3 tbsp. (50 mL) butter	1 tbsp. (15 mL) A-1 sauce
1 large onion, thinly sliced	1/4 tsp. (1 mL) thyme
1 small green pepper, slivered	A 1½ to 2-lb. (500 g to 1 kg) whole lamb liver
2 tbsp. (30 mL) chili sauce	1/3 cup (80 mL) Port or cold coffee

Preheat the convection section of your oven at 350°F (180°C). Melt the butter 3 minutes in an 8 x 8-inch (20 x 20 cm) ceramic dish or in a small metal saucepan of the same size, 2 minutes in the preheated oven.
Or melt the butter 2 minutes at HIGH, in a ceramic dish. Add the onion, stir well and cook 4 minutes at HIGH, the onion will brown lightly here and there. Stir, add the green pepper, stir and cook 1 minute at HIGH.
Place the low rack in the preheated 350°F (180°C) oven. Add the remaining ingredients to the onion and green pepper. Set the lamb liver in the center and baste with the vegetables and juice in the bottom of the dish.
Roast 30 to 40 minutes in the preheated oven. Let stand 10 minutes. Baste 7 or 8 times during that time. Slice thinly and serve with its sauce.

Lamb Meat Loaf

Microwave Cooking

This meat loaf may be served hot, but it is especially good cold. When cooked, cover it with waxed paper and place a weight over the paper. I have a brick which I keep for this purpose. Place a brick or a heavy object over the waxed paper, and cool. Refrigerate until ready to serve.

1½ lb (750 g) ground lamb	1 tsp. (5 mL) salt
1½ cups (375 mL) cooked rice	1/2 tsp. (2 mL) sugar
1/2 cup (125 mL) tomato juice	1 small onion, chopped fine
2 eggs, lightly beaten	2 tbsp. (30 mL) chili sauce
2 garlic cloves, minced	4 slices of bacon

Mix all the ingredients together except the bacon. Place in an 8 x 4 x 2½-inch (20 x 10 x 6.25 cm) loaf pan. Pack down. Place the bacon slices on top. Cook 10 minutes at HIGH. Cook another 10 minutes at MEDIUM. Let stand 20 minutes. Cover with waxed paper and place a weight on top. Refrigerate when cooled.

Pork

Pork

Pork is the most inexpensive meat, and it also has so many possibilities to offer. Pork may be fresh or smoked, and cooked as roast, chops, steaks, etc. Its mild flavor blends well with sage, aniseed, fennel, fresh or seeds, Juniper berries, thyme, marjoram, garlic, onion, apples, etc. The choice is wide and varied.

Pork Cuts

The loin roast — is divided in two, the tenderloin end, the meaty part of the loin which contains most of the tenderloin and some bones; but it is also the least meaty part when the tenderloin is removed and is sold separately. Sold as chops with tenderloin.
- The second part is the mid-section of the loin, less meaty than the tenderloin end. It contains rib bones, T-shape bone and little or no tenderloin. It is sold as roast or chops.

The loin roast — rib end — This cut contains the ribs, a portion of the blade bone but no tenderloin. It is cut into roasts or chops.

The Tenderloin — is a choice cut, sometimes difficult to find. The pork tenderloin is long, lean, tapered and very tender. Whole, it may be roasted; cut in one-inch (2.5 cm) slices, flattened with a meat mallet for delicious tender grilled meat.

Shoulder Roast — More economical cut. It is sold fresh, whole or cut into cubes for stewing, or smoked and sold as picnic ham.

Chops — Butt shoulder chops contain part of the long bone and rib bones; they are good for braising.

Picnic shoulder chops — The arm chops, cut from the shoulder, are easy to recognize by the round bone at top left. These chops are more tender and make good pork steaks.

A Few Hints on Roasting Pork in a Microwave Oven

As for beef, there is first the buying of pork, and then the appropriate cooking of the cut to ensure flavor and tenderness.

In microwave cooking as for any other type of cooking, the weight, the shape of the piece of meat, the tenderness of the cut, all play an important role. Roasts and chops will be more tender and will brown better after a standing time at room temperature before cooking.

Pork Chops — Various cuts

Pork chops have always been a family favorite, and the price is usually reasonable. How do you buy pork chops? Well, first of all the meat should be firm, tender, pink in color, and have a good rim of fat. The bones should be porous and pink.

Chops come in various cuts. It is important to be able to recognize them as each varies in price and cooking method. Pork chops, like beef, are cut from the loin and also the rib end of the loin. The back ribs (spare-ribs) are baked or barbecued, or cooked in the microwave oven, in a sweet and sour sauce.

How to defrost pork

I may be of the old school, but I still prefer defrosting roasts by placing them, wrapped, in a cool place for 10 to 12 hours, or 24 hours in the refrigerator. Then, I let the meat stand for 1 or 2 hours on the kitchen counter... the meat relaxes, fibers become tender, excess moisture evaporates, roasts and chops are always perfect. However, if you wish to or if you must, use your microwave for defrosting.

Well-thawed pork will feel cold to the touch, the fat will be shiny. Rolled roasts take longer to defrost than bone-in roasts.

It is important to turn boneless rolled roasts twice during the defrosting process.

If the piece of meat is irregularly shaped with tips of bones visible, they must be shielded with a strip of aluminum foil, to prevent the meat next to the bones from drying out, and consequently becoming tough.

How to defrost roasts

Count approximately 10 to 12 minutes per pound (20 to 25 minutes per kg), at DEFROST. Place wrapped roast in the microwave tray, defrost for half the required time.
Unwrap the meat. Check whether some spots are warmer, and cover with a piece of foil.
Turn roast, place on a microwave rack, and continue defrosting according to time recommended on chart.
I like to insert a wire tester in the middle of the roast to ensure that it is completely defrosted.
Cover with a cloth and let stand 20 to 30 minutes before roasting.

How to defrost chops, meat cubes for stewing and ground pork

- Defrost at DEFROST cycle, 4 to 8 minutes per pound (10 to 20 minutes per kg).
- Place the frozen meat in the microwave oven for half the time required at DEFROST cycle.
- Unwrap and break meat apart.
- Let stand at room temperature for 1 hour to defrost completely, or set in a plate and return to microwave for 1 or 2 minutes at DEFROST cycle.
  At that stage, it is easy to break up remaining meat balls, the meat should be pink, the fat white, because if it is transparent this would mean it is starting to cook.

How to defrost fresh and smoked sausages

- Defrost 3 to 4 minutes per pound (6 to 10 minutes per kg) at DEFROST without unwrapping. Turn the package after one minute. The sausages are defrosted when they can be separated.

Microwave Pork Roasting Chart*

Bone-in loin of 3 to 5-lb (1.5 to 2.5 kg)
Boneless loin of 3 to 5-lb (1.5 to 2.5 kg)
Both cuts are roasted at MEDIUM — 13 to 15 minutes per pound (27 to 30 minutes per kg)

Shoulder:

Blade (Butt) of 3 to 5 lb (1.5 to 2.5 kg) at MEDIUM — 16 to 18 minutes per pound (40 minutes per kg)
Boneless shoulder — Same time as butt.
Fresh leg — Roast only one half at a time — either the shank or the upper end of the leg —
2.5 to 3 lb (1 to 1.5 kg) at MEDIUM, 16 to 18 minutes per pound (40 minutes per kg)

It is best to have pork roast rolled and boned for perfect cooking in the microwave oven; although they do cook well with the bones.

Pork Chops

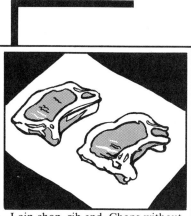

Loin chop, rib end. Chops without tenderloin.

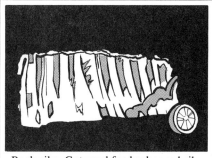

Back ribs. Cut used for barbecued ribs.

Loin ribs (country style), with backbone removed, to use as B.B.Q. pork rib — or slice to make small pork chops.

Loin chop, centre cut. Chops with tenderloin.

Roast of Pork Boulangère
Microwave Cooking

A meal-in-one. The roast cooks surrounded with potatoes and onions, all deliciously flavored with sage and marjoram. Without the potatoes and onions around the roast, you will have a microwave roast of pork. Serve with a gravy of your choice. (See Sauce chapter.)

A 3 to 4-lb (1.5 to 2 kg) roast of pork, boned and rolled

1 tsp. (5 mL) paprika

1 tbsp. (15 mL) vegetable oil

3 tbsp. (50 mL) fine breadcrumbs

1 tsp. (5 mL) sage

2 tbsp. (30 mL) butter

4 medium potatoes

4 medium onions

1 bay leaf

1/2 tsp. (2 mL) marjoram

1 tsp. (5 mL) salt

1/2 tsp. (2 mL) fresh ground pepper

Mix together the paprika, vegetable oil, breadcrumbs and sage. Roll the roast in this mixture. Preheat a browning dish (Corning) 7 minutes at HIGH. Set the roast in it, fat side down, without removing the dish from the oven. Brown 6 minutes at HIGH. Turn the roast and cook 25 minutes at MEDIUM. Remove the roast from the dish. Melt the butter in the dish, 1 minute at HIGH. Add the potatoes and onions, peeled and thinly sliced. Add the bay leaf, marjoram, salt and pepper. Mix well and place in a circular pattern around the dish. Place the roast in the middle. Roast, uncovered, 20 minutes at MEDIUM-HIGH. Let stand 15 minutes before serving.

Pork Roast "Fines Herbes"
Convection

Your oven may offer you convection cooking under a different name, for instance, Insta-matic. This is why I emphasize the importance of clearly understanding the operation manual.

A 3 to 4-lb (1.5 to 2 kg) pork loin roast, boned

2 tbsp. (30 mL) flour

3 tbsp. (50 mL) vegetable oil

1 tsp. (5 mL) paprika

1/4 tsp. (1 mL) each thyme and oregano

1/2 tsp. (2 mL) fennel seeds or aniseed

1/4 tsp. (1 mL) black pepper

1/2 tsp. (2 mL) salt

Mix the flour with the remaining ingredients which will give you a light batter. Baste the top and sides of the roast with it.

Place the spatter shield in the bottom of your oven, cover with the low rack. Place a pie plate under the rack (or follow directions in your operation manual). Roast at 350°F (180°C) 1 hour and 30 minutes.

Remove roast from the oven, set on a hot dish. Cover and let stand 20 minutes.

Remove rack. To the juice accumulated in the plate, add 1/3 cup (80 mL) cold coffee or tea or red wine. Stir well, crushing the small brown particles which add color and flavor to the gravy. Heat 2 minutes at HIGH and serve with the roast.

Pork Loin "Maison"
Convection

Roasted according to the convection method, the loin of pork is well browned and delicious. It is equally good hot or cold. It may be roasted with the bone or boned and rolled

A 3-lb (1.5 kg) loin of pork, boned and rolled

1 cup (250 mL) fine breadcrumbs

2 tsp. (10 mL) paprika

1 tsp. (5 mL) savory

1 tsp. (5 mL) salt

1/2 tsp. (2 mL) garlic powder

2 tbsp. (30 mL) melted margarine

1 egg white, lightly beaten

1 tbsp. (15 mL) cold water

Mix together the breadcrumbs, paprika, savory, salt, garlic powder and pepper. Add the melted margarine. Mix the egg white and the cold water in another bowl.
Place the spatter shield in the ceramic tray, place the broiling rack and then place a pie plate between the two. Or follow directions given in your oven operation manual for setting the racks. Preheat oven at 375°F (190°C) for 15 minutes. Roll the roast in the egg white and then in the breadcrumbs mixture. When the oven is hot, set the roast on the rack and roast at 375°F (190°C) 18 minutes per pound (36 minutes per kg). When cooked, place the roast on a hot dish, cover and let stand 15 minutes.

Gravy
Add the juice accumulated in the plate, 1/2 cup (125 mL) of either apple juice, cider, cold tea or white wine. Stir well while scraping the bottom of the plate. Add 1 tsp. (5 mL) cornstarch or flour. Mix well and cook 2 minutes at HIGH in the microwave. Stir and serve.

Loin of Pork, Kentish
With Temperature Probe

This is an old English recipe which I cook in the microwave oven, following the roasting method with a temperature probe (see your oven operation manual on how to use the probe, if you have one). In my oven, I use C.5 indicated for pork. The oven then takes over as to cooking time.

1/2 cup (125 mL) sherry

1/4 cup (60 mL) brown sugar

grated rind of one orange

1/3 cup (80 mL) orange juice

1 tsp. (5 mL) prepared horseradish

1 tsp. (5 mL) prepared mustard

A 4-lb (2 kg) loin of pork

Place the first 6 ingredients in a 4-cup (1 L) measure. Heat 3 minutes at HIGH. Place the roast in a 9 x 13-inch (22.5 x 32.5 cm) glass or ceramic dish, with bones in the bottom. Pour the hot mixture over all. Place the spatter shield in the ceramic tray, add the low rack. Insert the temperature probe into the roast and plug to the oven. Touch the PORK setting and start the oven. The oven will decide as to the time.
When the meat is cooked, remove from dish, add 1/3 cup (80 mL) cold water to the cooking juice, stir well. Heat at HIGH 1 minute 30 seconds.

Normandy Loin of Pork
Microwave Cooking

A mixture of vegetables cooked with the roast, then put through the food processor, serves to thicken the gravy in place of flour. The mixture of the fat and the orange juice gives a delicate flavor to the whole.

A 3-lb (1.5 kg) loin of pork, boned	**1 tsp. (5 mL) thyme**
2 tbsp. (30 mL) butter	**2 tsp. (10 mL) salt**
2 medium onions, diced	**1/2 tsp. (2 mL) pepper**
3 medium carrots, peeled and diced	**1/4 cup (60 mL) Port wine**
1 leek, cleaned and sliced	**Juice and grated rind of 2 oranges**
1 garlic clove, minced	**1 orange, peeled and thinly sliced**
1 small parsnip, peeled and thinly sliced	

Melt the butter 3 minutes at HIGH in a 6-cup (3 L) dish. Place the roast in it, fat side down. Heat 5 minutes at HIGH. Remove roast from dish, place the minced vegetables in the baking dish, stir. Cook 5 minutes at HIGH, stirring once during the cooking. Add the thyme, salt, pepper, stir. Set the meat over the mixture, the bones touching the bottom of the dish. Add the Port wine, orange juice and rind. Cover and cook 30 minutes at MEDIUM. Check for doneness; if necessary cook 10 minutes more at MEDIUM.

When cooked, place the roast on a warm service dish, pour the vegetable mixture into a food processor or a blender and cream. Add 1/4 cup (60 mL) tea or water and the thin orange slices. Cover and cook 3 minutes at HIGH, stirring once halfway through the cooking. Pour a few spoonfuls over the roast. Serve remaining gravy in a sauceboat.

Boned and Rolled Loin of Pork with Mustard

Microwave Cooking

A 3 to 4-lb (1.5 to 2 kg) boned and rolled roast is the perfect cut for microwave roasting. The roast will be well browned and cooked to perfection. When possible, have meat stand one hour at room temperature before cooking.

A 3 to 4-lb (1.5 to 2 kg) loin roast, boned and rolled

2 tbsp. (30 mL) vegetable oil

1/2 cup (125 mL) fine breadcrumbs

2 tbsp. (30 mL) French mustard

1/4 tsp. (1 mL) pepper

1 tsp. (5 mL) paprika

2 garlic cloves, chopped fine

9 cloves

Pat the roast dry with absorbent paper.

Heat vegetable oil 4 minutes at HIGH in an 8 x 8-inch (20 x 20 cm) glass dish. Mix together the remaining ingredients, except the whole cloves. Spread part of the mixture over the raw parts of the meat. Do not spread any on the fat. Place the fat part of the roast in the hot fat. Cook 10 minutes at HIGH.

Turn the roast, fat on top, placing it on a microwave rack. Push the cloves into the fat. Cover the fat with the remaining breadcrumbs. Cook at MEDIUM 13 minutes per pound (27 minutes per kg). Set the roast on a platter. Cover with waxed paper and let stand 10 minutes before serving. Salt and carve.

Shoulder Chops with Sauerkraut
Microwave Cooking

Once in a while I love a good dish of sauerkraut. I learned to appreciate it during a stay in Strasbourg, where excellent sauerkraut is served. The following recipe is family fare, easy to prepare. The first time I cooked it in the microwave oven, it was through curiosity, but to my surprise, I had never tasted it so good.

4 slices bacon and	1 large onion, diced
4 arm pork chops, if possible	1 tsp. (5 mL) pepper
or	1/2 tsp. (2 mL) juniper berries
8 arm pork chops	1/2 tsp. (2 mL) aniseed
1½ lb (750 g) sauerkraut	1/2 tsp. (2 mL) coarse salt
or	1/3 cup (80 mL) water or beer or white wine
A 32-oz. (909 mL) jar sauerkraut with wine	4 to 6 medium potatoes

Place half the sauerkraut in an 8-cup (2 L) ceramic baking dish. Place on top, the bacon and chops or chops alone. Sprinkle the meat with the onion. Mix together the pepper, juniper berries, aniseed and salt. Sprinkle half over the meat. Cover with the remaining sauerkraut. Place the potatoes on top, half burying them in the sauerkraut. Sprinkle the remaining seasoning on top. Add the chosen liquid. Cover. Cook 40 minutes at MEDIUM-HIGH. Let stand 10 minutes in the oven or in a warm place and serve.

Chinese Pork Chops
Microwave Cooking

This dish inspired by Chinese cooking is delicious when prepared with thinly sliced pork chops, which are often offered on Special at our markets. Remove bones and cut in strips.

1 lb (500 g) thin chops or pork shoulder	A 10-oz. (284 mL) can pineapple chunks
2 tbsp. (30 mL) vegetable oil	1/2 cup (125 mL) barbecue or plum sauce
1 garlic clove, minced	1 tbsp. (15 mL) cornstarch
1 tsp. (5 mL) salt	2 tbsp. (30 mL) soy sauce
1/4 tsp. (1 mL) pepper	1 green pepper, slivered

Cut the meat on the bias into thin slices. Heat the vegetable oil 3 minutes at HIGH in an 8 x 8-in. (20 x 20 cm) ceramic dish. Place the meat in the hot oil. Mix well and cook 2 minutes at HIGH. Salt and pepper. Add the juice drained from the pineapple, the garlic and barbecue or Chinese plum sauce. Mix well. Cover and cook 15 minutes at MEDIUM. Mix the cornstarch with the soy sauce. Add to the meat together with the green pepper. Stir well and cook 5 minutes at MEDIUM-HIGH. Stir halfway through the cooking. Serve with boiled rice.

Roast of Pork with Sauerkraut (last photo back bottom)
Microwave Cooking

A favorite Alsatian dish. Use the cut of your choice. Personally, I prefer the bone-in pork rib. This dish reheats very well. I often cook it a day ahead, and then need only warm it up. Use the REHEAT cycle, if your oven has that cycle, or 10 to 20 minutes at MEDIUM. That is why I like to use a ceramic casserole to cook this dish.

A 3 to 4-lb (1.5 to 2 kg) pork roast

A 32-oz (909 mL) jar of sauerkraut with wine

2 onions, cut in four

1 garlic clove, finely chopped

1 tsp. (5 mL) salt

10 juniper berries (optional)

12 peppercorns

6 medium potatoes, peeled

1/2 cup (125 mL) white wine or water

Place the pork roast in a ceramic dish with cover. Mix the sauerkraut with the remaining ingredients, except the potatoes. Place all around the roast.
Add the white wine or water. Bury the potatoes at the top of the sauerkraut. Cover tightly and cook 1 hour and 15 minutes at MEDIUM. Let stand 20 minutes before serving.

Pork Shoulder Roasted in a Bag
Microwave Cooking

This is actually a braised roast. For lack of a cooking bag, the meat may be placed in a deep baking dish. Cover the dish with plastic wrap and cook according to the following recipe. Serve with frozen or canned corn kernels and mashed potatoes.

1 tsp. (5 mL) rosemary or sage

1/2 tsp. (2 mL) salt

1/4 tsp. (1 mL) pepper

A 4-lb (2 kg) boned pork shoulder

2 medium onions, cut in four

1 carrot, peeled and cut in four

3 sprigs of fresh parsley

1 leek, cut in three

1/2 cup (125 mL) white vermouth or chicken consommé

1 tbsp. (15 mL) cornstarch

1/2 cup (125 mL) cold water

Mix together the rosemary or sage, salt and pepper. Brush over the raw part of the meat. Place it in a plastic cooking bag. Add onions, carrot, parsley, leek and the white vermouth or consommé. Tie the bag with a string, not too tightly. With the point of a knife, make 2 or 3 incisions in the top of the bag. Put it in a 9 x 13-inch (22.5 x 32.5 cm) glass dish. Cook 15 minutes at HIGH. Move the bag while holding it with a cloth, so as to stir the juice inside. Cook 15 minutes per pound (500 g) at MEDIUM. Let the roast stand in the bag for 20 minutes.
Cut a corner of the bag with scissors to let the juice run into the baking dish. Place the roast on a platter without removing it from the bag. Keep in a warm place.
To the juice in the baking dish, add the cornstarch diluted in the cold water. Stir well and cook 1 minute at HIGH, stir and cook 1 minute more, if necessary, for a light transparent gravy. Place the roast and vegetables on a serving dish and serve hot with the hot gravy.

Spanish Roast of Pork *(photo opposite page 80)*
Microwave Cooking

A pork roast orange glazed halfway through cooking. I like to cook half a leg of fresh ham, butt end. Superb cold, it is like a glazed smoked ham, a fine piece for a buffet.

Half a leg of fresh ham, 3 to 4 lb (1.5 to 2 kg)

1/2 tsp. (2 mL) ground ginger

or

1 tbsp. (15 mL) fresh ginger, grated

1 tsp. (5 mL) paprika

Glaze:

1/2 cup (125 mL) marmalade

3/4 cup (200 mL) orange juice

grated rind of one orange

2 tbsp. (30 mL) cornstarch

1/2 tsp. (2 mL) salt

1/2 tsp. (2 mL) powdered ginger

1 cup (250 mL) fresh grapes, cut in half

1/3 cup (80 mL) orange liqueur or brandy, to your taste

Mix together the ground or fresh grated ginger and the paprika. Brush the top of the roast with the mixture. Set the roast on a microwave rack in a glass baking dish. Cook 30 minutes at MEDIUM. Mix the glaze ingredients in a 4-cup (1 L) measure. Remove roast from oven, and also the rack. Pour the glaze mixture into the baking dish. Cook 5 minutes at HIGH, stirring twice during the cooking. Return the roast to the baking dish, spoon the glaze over it for 1 or 2 minutes. Cover with plastic wrap. Cook another 30 minutes at MEDIUM, or until the thermometer registers 165°F (75°C). After 15 to 20 minutes standing time, covered with waxed paper, the temperature will rise to 170°F (80°C). Baste the roast 4 to 5 times with the glaze. Serve with parsleyed rice or a barley casserole.

Normandy Pork Chops
Microwave Cooking

In Normandy, a very high alcohol content cider is used, which I have replaced with brandy. Serve with wild rice or mashed potatoes.

6 one-inch (2.5 cm) thick pork chops	2 tbsp. (30 mL) butter
1/4 cup (60 mL) flour	8 to 12 prunes, pitted
1 tsp. (5 mL) salt	1 cup (250 mL) Port wine
1/4 tsp. (1 mL) pepper	2 tbsp. (30 mL) brandy
1/2 tsp. (2 mL) thyme	2 tbsp. (30 mL) whipping cream
1 tsp. (5 mL) paprika	

Mix together the flour, salt, pepper and thyme in a large plate. Roll the chops in the mixture to coat them well, sprinkle each one with paprika. Melt the butter in an 8 x 8-inch (20 x 20 cm) ceramic dish 3 minutes at HIGH. Add the chops. Cook 4 minutes at MEDIUM-HIGH, turn. Cover the dish with plastic wrap and cook the chops 20 minutes at MEDIUM. Check for doneness; if necessary cook another 5 minutes. In the interval, soak the pitted prunes 15 minutes in hot water. Drain thoroughly. Add the Port wine to the prunes and heat together 4 minutes at HIGH.
Remove the chops from the dish, keep in a warm place, and add the brandy to the juice. Heat 1 minute at HIGH. Add the prune juice and the cream. Mix together, heat 3 minutes at HIGH. Add the prunes. Heat 2 minutes at HIGH. Serve in a sauceboat or set the prunes around the chops and serve the juice in a sauceboat.

Make the most of a Loin of Pork

Take a 4-lb (2 kg) bone-in pork loin roast.

To get the most out of it, cut it up in the following manner:
a) Bone the roast, use the bones for Bavarian Sauerkraut Dumplings.
b) Remove 2 chops, mince to be used in a spaghetti sauce.
c) Roll and tie remaining roast, cook by convection at 165°F (78°C), with baked potatoes.
Add a 1-lb (500 g) pork loin; it will give 4 to 6 servings, stir-frying it.

Boiled Ham
Microwave Cooking

This is an old recipe from the repertoire of Québec cuisine. One day, out of curiosity, I tried to adapt it to microwave cooking. It was such a success that my family and I vowed that we would always boil ham in this manner.

A 4-lb (2 kg) shoulder of ham
or
a half-ham of 4 to 6 lb (2 to 3 kg)
1 bay leaf
10 peppercorns
6 whole allspice cloves

2 large onions, quartered
2 carrots, sliced
1 bunch of celery leaves
1 tbsp. (15 mL) dry mustard
1/2 cup (125 mL) molasses
boiling water

Be sure to choose a baking dish that will hold enough water to completely or almost completely cover the ham. Remove the glycin casing and the net around the ham, if necessary. Place the ham in the dish with all the ingredients. Pour boiling water over all to at least almost cover the ham. If your dish has a cover, use it, or cover with plastic wrap.
As to cooking time, you must know the exact weight of the meat cut. Cook 10 minutes per pound (500 g) at HIGH.
When the ham is cooked, remove the rind and turn the ham so the top part will be submerged.
Cool 4 to 5 hours in the cooking water. Remove from the water, cover with a bowl or a plastic sheet and refrigerate 5 to 6 hours, should you wish to serve it cold.
To serve it hot, let stand 30 minutes in its cooking water, set on a serving platter and serve.

Orange-glazed Ham Steak *(last photo front)*
Microwave Cooking

One of my favorite ham dishes. It is quickly prepared, and very attractive with a 2-inch (5 cm) thick ham slice. Excellent as a hot or cold buffet dish.

1/2 cup (125 mL) brown sugar
1 tbsp. (15 mL) cornstarch
1 tsp. (1 mL) curry powder
1/2 cup (125 mL) fresh orange juice

grated rind of 2 oranges
1 ham slice, 1 to 2 inches (2.5 to 5 cm) thick
6 cloves

In a 12 x 9-inch (30 x 22.5 cm) glass baking dish, combine brown sugar, cornstarch and curry powder. Stir in the orange juice and rind. Mix well. Place the ham slice over the mixture, turn it around two or three times to coat it well on both sides. Stud the fat with the cloves here and there. Cook 10 minutes at MEDIUM, uncovered. Move the ham slice and spoon with the sauce halfway through the cooking. Cover and cook 10 minutes at MEDIUM. Let stand 5 minutes, covered. Set the ham on a platter, stir the sauce and use to glaze the top of the ham slice. Very interesting surrounded with cranberry sauce.

Spanish Roast of Pork (p. 78) →

Bavarian Sauerkraut Dumplings

1 large can sauerkraut, of your choice

2 medium onions, chopped

Bones from roast*

2 garlic cloves, minced

1 tsp. (5 mL) salt

1 tsp. (5 mL) dill seeds

1½ cups (375 mL) water or white wine

Make layers of sauerkraut, onions, garlic and bones in slow-cooker. Spray each row with some of the salt and dill seeds mixed together. Pour water on top. Cover with perforated top and glass cover. Cook 30 to 35 minutes at HIGH.

Meanwhile, prepare the dumplings.

Mix in a bowl:

1½ cups (375 mL) all-purpose flour

1 tsp. (5 mL) dried parsley

1 tsp. (5 mL) summer savory

2 tsp. (10 mL) baking powder

1/2 tsp. (2 mL) salt

Mix a second bowl:

2/3 cup (160 mL) milk

1 egg

2 tbsp. (30 mL) vegetable oil

Mix the two together only when ready to cook.

To cook:

Remove meat from dish. Mix dumplings. Place on top of sauerkraut by spoonfuls. Cover and cook 5 to 6 minutes at HIGH.

* *Ask your butcher to give you the bones removed from the 4-lb (2 kg) loin of pork, or use 2-lb (1 kg) pork spareribs.*

← Top: Fore Shanks with Beer (p. 63)
← Bottom: Lamb Chops Maison (p. 60)

Alsatian Poached Ham
Microwave Cooking

It may be served hot or cold. There are very few ways of poaching a ham that could equal this Alsatian method and give you such a flavorful and tender ham.

1/4 cup (60 mL) butter or margarine

2 medium carrots, peeled and thinly sliced

2 leeks, washed and thinly sliced

1 large onion, thinly sliced

2 branches of celery, diced

A 3 to 5-lb (1.5 to 2.5 kg) pre-cooked ham

2 cups (500 mL) white wine or dry cider or light beer

4 cloves

4 tbsp. (60 mL) brown sugar

3 tbsp. (50 mL) cornstarch

2 tbsp. (30 mL) rum or brandy

Melt the butter 3 minutes at HIGH in an 8-cup (2 L) ceramic baking dish. Add the carrots, leeks, onion and celery. Mix well. Cook 5 minutes at HIGH. Stir together and set the ham on this bed of vegetables. Add the remaining ingredients, except the cornstarch, rum or brandy.
Roll the ham in the mixture, cover and cook 30 minutes at MEDIUM. Turn the ham halfway through the cooking. Let stand 20 minutes, covered. Remove the ham from the dish. Strain the juice and pour it into the baking dish. Mix together the cornstarch and rum or brandy. Stir into the juice. Cook 4 to 5 minutes at MEDIUM-HIGH, stirring twice during cooking. When cooked, the gravy will be creamy, light and transparent. Pour into a sauceboat and warm up as needed before serving.
Another way, to serve the ham cold, is to place it in a large dish, pour the cooked gravy on top and baste the ham many times with the gravy during the next 15 to 20 minutes, this will form a glaze on top of the ham.

Ham Loaf
Convection Method

I serve it cold, very thinly sliced, with a salad of cucumbers and white onions, marinated two hours in a French dressing to taste.

1½-lb (750 g) ground ham, raw or cooked

1/4-lb (125 g) ground pork

3 eggs, lightly beaten

1/2 cup (125 mL) cream of celery soup, undiluted

1/2 tsp. (2 mL) marjoram or curry

1/2 tsp. (2 mL) dry mustard

1 cup (250 mL) fine breadcrumbs

Mix all the ingredients together in the order given. Pack well into a 9 x 5-inch (22.5 x 13 cm) bread pan. Place the browning rack over the ceramic tray.
Preheat oven to 350°F (180°C) 15 minutes. Place the meat loaf on the rack. Bake 30 to 40 minutes or until the meat loaf is golden brown.

Honey-glazed Half Ham (photo opposite page 97 top)
Microwave cooking

This ham is perfect when prepared with a ham that is not pre-cooked. Read the label carefully for instructions. This recipe may be prepared with half a leg of ham or with a small whole shoulder.

A 4 to 5-lb (2 to 2.5 kg) shoulder or leg of ham

1/2 cup (125 mL) brown sugar

a cinnamon stick

6 cloves

10 peppercorns

6 whole allspice

1 small onion, peeled and cut in four

Remove casing from ham. Place it in a plastic cooking bag and add all the ingredients. Tie with a wet string or a strip cut off the top of the bag. Do not tighten the bag too much around the ham. Make a slit with the tip of a knife on top of the bag. Set in a 12 x 7-inch (30 x 18 cm) glass dish. Cook 10 minutes at HIGH. Continue cooking for 35 minutes at MEDIUM. Turn bag halfway through cooking. When cooked, remove ham from the bag and place it on the baking dish. Remove the rind, if need be. Spoon the following glaze over the ham.

The Glaze:

1/2 cup (125 mL) honey

1 tbsp. (15 mL) cider vinegar

1 tsp. (5 mL) cornstarch

grated rind of one orange

juice of half an orange

Place all the ingredients in a 4-cup (1 L) measure cup. Cook 2 minutes at HIGH. Stir and spread over the ham. Baste 5 or 6 times. Cook 4 to 5 minutes at MEDIUM, basting the ham with the sauce 3 times during the cooking. Remove from oven and continue basting 5 or 6 times. Serve hot or cold.

Yorkshire Sausages
Convection

Nice golden sausages in a pancake very easily unmolded... the perfect dish for a brunch or light meal. These are cooked by the convection method.

6 to 8 pork sausages

3 eggs, lightly beaten

1 cup (250 mL) milk

1/2 cup (125 mL) flour

1/2 tsp. (2 mL) salt

1/4 tsp. (1 mL) savory or curry

paprika

Place the sausages in a dish. Cover with hot water (tap water will do). Cook 5 minutes at HIGH. Drain thoroughly. Mix together the eggs, milk, flour, salt and savory or curry, to obtain a nice smooth batter. Set the sausages in a 9-inch (22.5 cm) pie plate. Cover with the batter. Sprinkle lightly with paprika. Place on a browning rack. Cook at 425°F (220°C) for 20 to 25 minutes or until the pancake is all puffy and the sausages well browned.

Sausage and Corn Pancake
Convection

This pancake can be made with half a pound or one pound (250 or 500 g) sausages. Serve with a green salad. You will have a complete meal, easily prepared.

1 lb (500 g) sausages of your choice

A 12-oz. (341 mL) can of whole kernel corn

2 eggs, lightly beaten

4 green onions or 1 small onion, chopped

2/3 cup (160 mL) soda crackers, crushed

3 tbsp. (50 mL) parsley, minced

1 tsp. (5 mL) marjoram

1/4 tsp. (1 mL) pepper

1 tsp. (5 mL) salt

Place the sausages in a dish and cover with hot water. Cook 10 minutes at HIGH. Drain thoroughly and place the sausages in a deep 9-inch (22.5 cm) pie plate.
Drain the corn, reserving the liquid, and pour the corn over the sausages. Add enough milk to the reserved liquid to have 1½ cups (375 mL) in all. Add the remaining ingredients, mix well. Pour over the sausages. Cook in the convection oven preheated at 350°F (180°C), 35 to 45 minutes or until the pancake is puffed and golden.

Sausages, scrambled eggs and browned potatoes *(last photo back top)*

Microwave Cooking

Excellent lunch, nutritious, quick and easy.

2 medium potatoes	**salt and pepper**
1/2 lb (250 g) sausages	**1 tbsp. (15 mL) butter**
4 eggs	**green onions or minced parsley**

Scrub the potatoes. Make one or two incisions into each one with the point of a knife. Place on a microwave rack. Cook 5 to 6 minutes at HIGH. Cool.*
Sprinkle the sausages with paprika. Place in an 8 x 8-inch (20 x 20 cm) baking dish and cook 5 to 6 minutes at HIGH. Turn the sausages halfway through the cooking, finish cooking. Sausages will then be browned here and there. Place on a warm serving platter. Keep in a warm place.
Peel the potatoes, dice, sprinkle with paprika and green onions. Mix and pour into the sausage cooking fat. Mix together and place in the shape of a crown around the dish. Cook 5 minutes at HIGH. Stir well and add the sausages. Melt the butter 1 minute at HIGH in the middle of the dish. Break the eggs into it. Prick each yolk and each white with the point of a knife. Cover the dish with plastic wrap or waxed paper. Cook at MEDIUM 1 minute for each egg or a little more if you wish. Serve with the sausages and potatoes.

* Potatoes already cooked can also be used.

Stir-fried Pork Tenderloin

1/4 cup (60 mL) toasted sesame seeds	**4 - 6 green onions, chopped**
A small pork tenderloin	**1 tbsp. (15 mL) vegetable oil**
1 tbsp. (15 mL) water	**1 or 2 garlic cloves, minced**
1/4 cup (60 mL) soy sauce (Kikkoman)	**2 tbsp. (30 mL) minced ginger root**

Spread sesame seeds in an 8 x 8 inch (20 x 20 cm) ceramic or glass dish. Toast at HIGH 3 to 5 minutes, stirring often and taking out as soon as seeds are golden brown. Set aside in small dish and reserve. Place whole tenderloin in dish. Combine remaining ingredients and pour over tenderloin. Cover, cook at HIGH 5 to 8 minutes. Baste pork. Cover and cook 3 minutes at HIGH. Stir and serve, thinly sliced.

Pork Chops or Steak
Microwave Cooking

The same recipe may be followed for a pork steak or for chops. Only the cooking time varies. For chops over one inch (2.5 cm) thick, add 3 minutes more at MEDIUM-HIGH.

4 loin or rib pork chops, 1 inch (2.5 cm) thick

1 tbsp. (15 mL) vegetable oil

1 tsp. (5 mL) paprika

1 tsp. (5 mL) savory or sage

1/2 tsp. (2 mL) salt

1/4 tsp. (1 mL) pepper

1/2 tsp. (2 mL) sugar

Preheat an 8 x 8-inch (20 x 20 cm) browning dish (Corning) 7 minutes at HIGH. Mix the remaining ingredients together. Dip one side of the chops into the mixture, using your fingers to make it stick to the meat. Place the chops in the hot browning dish, without removing it from the oven, the flavored side in the bottom. Brown 4 minutes at HIGH. Turn the chops and finish cooking 3 minutes at MEDIUM-HIGH. Let stand 3 minutes and serve.

Cooked Pork Risotto
Microwave Cooking

A few minutes of cooking with no effort using one or two cups (250 - 500 mL) already cooked leftover pork, and you have a meal for four people.

1 to 2 cups (250 to 500 mL) cooked pork, thinly sliced or diced

1/3 cup (80 mL) chili sauce

1/4 tsp. (1 mL) salt

1 tsp. (5 mL) celery seeds

1/4 tsp. (1 mL) nutmeg

3 tbsp. (50 mL) cider or wine vinegar

1 bay leaf

1 cup (250 mL) water

1/2 cup (125 mL) long grain rice

Place the pork in a glass baking dish of your choice. Mix the remaining ingredients together, pour over the meat. Cover and cook 20 minutes at MEDIUM-HIGH, stirring once during the cooking.

Roasted Boneless Loin of Pork

With Temperature Probe

A 3 to 4-lb (1.5 to 2 kg) boned and rolled loin
   roast

3 tbsp. (50 mL) bacon fat or margarine

1 tsp. (5 mL) dry mustard

1 garlic clove, minced

1/4 tsp. (1 mL) black pepper

1 tsp. (5 mL) savory or sage

6 potatoes

1 tsp. (5 mL) coarse salt

Cream together the bacon fat or margarine, mustard, garlic, black pepper, savory or sage. Spread on top of roast.

Place spatter shield in ceramic tray, top with low baking rack, place ceramic pie plate under baking rack.

Set roast on rack, insert probe in top of oven and in meat, press C5. The oven decides the cooking period. Read instructions in your oven manual, if it has a prober. Let stand 15 minutes, covered.* Rub potatoes with a little fat, then roll in coarse salt. Place around the roast.

* This roast cooks by convection with "Probe". Study the instructions in your oven manual for this type of cooking, which could differ slightly. It is easy to adapt as the preparation does not change.

Broiled Sausages

Microwave Cooking

Once you have tasted pork sausages cooked in the microwave oven, you will no longer wish to cook them in the frying pan.

1/2 lb (250 g) pork sausages

paprika and garlic salt

a pinch of savory, to taste

Preheat an 8 x 8-in. (20 x 20 cm) browning dish (Corning) 7 minutes at HIGH. Sprinkle the sausages with paprika and garlic salt. Place them in the hot dish, without removing it from the oven. Broil 2 minutes at HIGH. Holding the dish by the two handles, move it back and forth to turn the sausages. Cook another 2 minutes at HIGH. Serve.

Spaghetti Sauce

2 pork chops, minced	1 carrot, grated
2 medium onions, minced	1/2 tsp. (2 mL) basil or oregano
2 celery sticks, diced	1 bay leaf

Place all the ingredients in a 4-cup (1 L) casserole. Cook at HIGH 8 minutes, stirring twice.
Add:

A 19-oz. (540 mL) can tomatoes

1 tsp. (5 mL) salt

1 tsp. (5 mL) sugar

1/2 tsp. (2 mL) pepper

Stir well and cook at HIGH 4 minutes.
This sauce is sufficient to serve with 8 ounces (250 mL) cooked spaghetti.

Sauces and their magic

Sauces and their Magic

There is almost no limit to the number of ingredients, both cooked and uncooked, that can be mixed together to create delicious sauces. Once you have mastered the best-known classic sauces, some methods of preparing them and the basic ingredients, you will be able to use your imagination to develop other variations.

The perfect sauce enhances both the appearance and the flavor of the food with which it is served. Herbs, extracts, spices and salt do not change the basic recipe; using more or less than is called for will not change the texture of your sauce. The consistency can be made thicker or thinner, too.

If, because of time involved, you have never bothered much with sauces, you will soon change your habits with a microwave oven since it completely eliminates the difficulty, extra care and work required to prepare a sauce. Lumps, burning, constant stirring, all are eliminated. You may even prepare some sauces ahead of time, refrigerate them or keep them at room temperature, for quick reheating when needed. You will quickly learn how to adapt your own favorite sauce to microwave cooking. The important thing is to stir a sauce thoroughly, even two or three times during the cooking, and to use your own common sense as to the time required. For example: if your white sauce recipe calls for a 5-minute cooking period at HIGH, and the milk, butter and flour are very cold, or should the butter be soft and the milk at room temperature, then there may be a 1 or 2-minute variation in cooking time. Alternatively, should you prefer to proceed more slowly and cook the sauce at MEDIUM, then 2 to 4 minutes more will be required than at HIGH.

Do not be afraid to open the oven door to check the cooking, as residual heat remains in the ingredients while you are stirring.

Sauces are important in good cuisine. They garnish, extend or bind together the food you are serving and, of course they enhance the flavor.

The Finishing Touches to a Perfect Roast

Three ways to make gravy
1. A creamy sauce, obtained by the addition of flour.
2. A clear sauce, made by adding a cold liquid to the fat in the pan.
3. The perfect gravy, made by adding a can of cold undiluted consommé to the hot fat in the dripping pan, for more flavor and color.

Good flour gravy has an appetizing color.

Add the flour to the fat in the pan, stir well, cook 2 minutes at HIGH, and stir again.

The perfect proportions for a flour gravy are 2 tablespoons (30 mL) of fat to 2 tablespoons (30 mL) of flour. If you use more than 2 tablespoons of fat, the gravy always separates and becomes greasy. Use 1/2 cup (125 mL) of liquid for each tablespoon of flour.

The liquid used to make a clear gravy makes a big difference. It is not a set rule that you must use cold water. Leftover tea or coffee, tomato juice, milk, cream, wine, etc., will give a completely different flavor and color.

Notes on Sauces and their Variations

Flour or other starch with cold liquid
The liquid can be cold water, milk, wine, vegetable or fruit juice, consommé, and the starch can be any flour such as wheat or potato flour, cornstarch or fine tapioca. Each kind will give a slightly different texture to the finished sauce. Whichever liquid you use, and it must be cold, the preparation is the same, you add the starch to it, stir to a smooth cream or thin paste, then add to boiling stock or gravy or water. Beat with a wire whisk until thoroughly blended. To obtain a smooth, creamy texture free from any starchy flavor, cook the mixture for 1 to 3 minutes at MEDIUM-HIGH, stirring to mix after each minute of cooking, until you have the desired consistency.

The usual proportion of flour to liquid for a flour-thickened sauce is 2 teaspoons (10 mL) flour to

1/2 cup (125 mL) liquid, although some recipes call for different amounts. To substitute another starch for the 2 teaspoons (10 mL) wheat flour, use any one of the following: 1 teaspoon (5 mL) cornstarch, 1⅔ teaspoons (8 mL) rice flour, 2/3 teaspoon (3 mL) potato flour or arrowroot.

How to make a Sauce velouté

The liquid which accumulates in the plate under the roast is called a "fumet"; as an average there usually is from 3/4 to 1 cup (200 to 250 mL).

To make the velouté

Remove to a dish 3 tablespoons (50 mL) of the fat accumulated in the plate, add 2 tablespoons (30 mL) of flour, stir, cook 1 minute at MEDIUM-HIGH, stirring twice during cooking.

Put the remaining "fumet" accumulated in the plate in a measuring cup, add enough chicken or beef consommé, or cream, or light white wine, to make up 1 to 1½ cups (250 to 375 mL) of liquid. Flavor will vary with each liquid used. Stir thoroughly, add the starch mixed with the 3 tablespoons (50 mL) of fat. Mix well and cook 2 to 3 minutes at HIGH. Stir once or twice, preferably with a whisk, to obtain a smooth creamy texture. Salt and pepper to taste.

Basic Brown Sauce

1/2 cup (125 mL) chopped celery

1/2 cup (125 mL) chopped carrots

1/2 cup (125 mL) chopped onion

1/4 tsp. (1 mL) dried thyme

1 bay leaf

1/4 tsp. (1 mL) dried marjoram, savory or
tarragon

3 tbsp. (50 mL) roast fat

4 tbsp. (60 mL) flour

2 cups (500 mL) beef stock

or

The "fumet accumulated under the roast
PLUS water, or white or red wine (white with
white meat and red with red meat) to make
up 2 cups (500 mL) of liquid

First prepare the vegetables, then add the herbs.

Remove the 3 tablespoons (50 mL) fat from the "fumet", stir in the vegetables and the herbs with a wooden spoon, add 2 tablespoons (30 mL) water. Cook 3 minutes at HIGH, stirring once during cooking.

Sprinkle the softened vegetables with the flour and stir until well mixed. Cook 3 to 4 minutes at HIGH or until small brown spots appear here and there. Add 1 teaspoon (5 mL) Kitchen Bouquet or 1/2 teaspoon (2 mL) molasses. Add the chosen liquid, stir to blend well, season to taste, cook 5 minutes at MEDIUM-HIGH, stirring once or twice during cooking.

Variations of the Basic Brown Sauce

Sauce Robert
For roasted pork, or to warm up beef and root vegetables.
Instead of the 3 vegetables and herbs, of the basic brown sauce, use only 4 chopped onions. Flavor with 1/4 teaspoon (1 mL) dried thyme and the grated rind of 1 lemon. Use 1/2 cup (125 mL) white wine to replace 1/2 cup (125 mL) of the liquid. When the sauce is finished, flavor it with 1 teaspoon (5 mL) of Dijon mustard.

Sauce piquante
For roasted veal, all pork dishes and all chops.
Instead of the vegetables of the basic brown sauce, use only onions, as in sauce Robert. Flavor with 1 bay leaf and 1/4 teaspoon (1 mL) salt. Replace 1/4 cup (60 mL) of the liquid with 1/4 cup (60 mL) cider vinegar, and add 1 teaspoon (5 mL) sugar. When the sauce is finished, add 4 tablespoons (60 mL) thinly sliced baby gherkins.

Sauce espagnole
Add 2 minced garlic cloves and a generous amount of freshly ground pepper to the vegetables of the basic brown sauce. When the vegetables are soft and translucent, add 2 tablespoons (30 mL) tomato paste. Finish the sauce in the usual fashion.

Sauce madère or Madeira sauce
For all roasted meats and for boiled ham.
Add 1/4 cup (60 mL) dry Madeira to the 2 cups (500 mL) liquid of the basic brown sauce, or substitute 1/2 cup (125 mL) Madeira for 1/2 cup (125 mL) of the liquid.

Sauce Chasseur
Serve with veal, ground meat, meat loaf, etc.

4 green onions, chopped

2 tbsp. (30 mL) butter

1 cup (250 mL) fresh or well drained
  canned tomatoes

1 small garlic clove

1/4 tsp. (1 mL) salt

1/2 tsp. (2 mL) basil

1/2 tsp. (2 mL) sugar

1/2 cup (125 mL) white wine

1 cup (250 mL) basic brown sauce

1/4 lb (125 g) mushrooms, thinly sliced

2 tbsp. (30 mL) butter

Place the green onions in a dish and cook 3 minutes at HIGH, stirring once.
Peel or drain and dice the tomatoes, add to the onions together with the garlic, basil, sugar and salt.
Cover and cook 5 minutes at MEDIUM.
Add the wine and the basic brown sauce. Stir well and cook 5 minutes at MEDIUM.
In a separate dish, melt the 2 tablespoons (30 mL) butter 1 minute at HIGH. Add the mushrooms, mix well and cook 2 minutes at HIGH. Stir well. Add to the brown sauce. Taste for seasoning. If necessary, heat 1 minute at HIGH.

Devilled Sauce

4 green onions, chopped

1 tbsp. (15 mL) butter

1 cup (250 mL) white wine or
  2/3 cup (160 mL) French vermouth

Fresh ground pepper

2 cups (500 mL) basic brown sauce

Place the green onions and the butter in a baking dish, cook 2 minutes at HIGH. Mix well, add the wine or vermouth, cook 3 minutes at HIGH. Stir and cook 2 more minutes at HIGH, or until the wine is almost totally reduced. Add the basic brown sauce and cook 2 minutes at MEDIUM, stir well and serve.

Chef's Brown Sauce

1/2 tsp. (2 mL) sugar

1 small onion, chopped

3 tbsp. (50 mL) butter

2 tbsp. (30 mL) flour

A 10-oz. (284 mL) can beef broth, undiluted

1/8 tsp. (0.5 mL) thyme

1 bay leaf

1/4 cup (60 mL) milk

1/2 cup (125 mL) dry skim milk

1/4 cup (60 mL) water

2 tsp. (10 mL) tomato paste

Place the sugar and onion in a 4-cup (1 L) bowl. Cook, uncovered, 2 minutes at HIGH, or until sugar is partially browned. Add butter. Cook, uncovered, 1 minute at HIGH. Mix well. Stir in flour, blend well, add beef broth, thyme, bay leaf and the 1/4 cup (60 mL) milk. Mix well, then cook, uncovered, 1 minute at HIGH. Stir well, add dry milk, water and tomato paste, blend well. Cook, uncovered, 2 to 3 minutes at HIGH, or until sauce is creamy, stirring once during cooking.

Simplified Brown Sauce

If you like a lot of gravy, make this sauce, which is easy to prepare. It will keep 8 to 10 days refrigerated.

1/4 cup (60 mL) minced onion	1/8 tsp. (0.5 mL) pepper
1/2 tsp. (125 mL) sugar	1/4 tsp. (1 mL) thyme
2 tbsp. (30 mL) butter	1 bay leaf
2 tbsp. (30 mL) flour	2 tsp. (10 mL) tomato paste
2 cups (500 mL) canned beef consommé*	

Cook the onion and the sugar in the butter 2 minutes at HIGH. Stir well and cook 1 minute more, if necessary, for the onions to start browning slightly here and there. Add the flour, stir well. Add the consommé, pepper, thyme, bay leaf and tomato paste. Cook 10 minutes at MEDIUM-HIGH, stirring three times during the cooking.

* Add enough water to the consommé to have 2 cups (500 mL) of liquid.

Sauce Robert with Simplified Brown Sauce

1 tbsp. (15 mL) butter	1 recipe simplified brown sauce
1 tbsp. (15 mL) vegetable oil	3 to 4 tsp. (15 - 20 mL) Dijon mustard
1 onion, minced	3 tbsp. (50 mL) soft butter
1 cup (250 mL) white wine	3 tbsp. (50 mL) parsley, minced

Place the butter, vegetable oil and onion in a baking dish, mix well, add the wine, stir and cook 5 to 8 minutes at HIGH, stirring three times during the cooking. The wine must reduce without the onion drying up.
Heat the brown sauce 1 minute at HIGH. Add the reduced wine. Mix together the mustard, soft butter and minced parsley, add to the sauce and stir to mix well. Heat 1 minute at HIGH, stir well and serve.

Quick Madeira or Port Sauce

1/4 cup (60 mL) Madeira or Port wine

1 recipe of simplified brown sauce

2 tbsp. (30 mL) butter

Add the Madeira or Port wine to the simplified brown sauce, cook 5 minutes at MEDIUM-HIGH, stirring three times during the cooking. Remove from oven. Add the butter, stir until the butter has melted.

Basting Sauce for Roasts

Use to baste any roast, or use on microwave broiled steak, or over chicken, duck or lamb. One or two bastings during the cooking should be sufficient to give a very interesting flavor to the meat.

1 garlic clove, halved

1/2 cup (125 mL) each of lemon juice and vegetable oil

2 tsp. (10 mL) marjoram or basil

1/2 tsp. (2 mL) fresh ground pepper

2 tsp. (10 mL) salt

1/3 cup (80 mL) Worcestershire sauce

Place the ingredients in a glass jar. Close the jar, shake vigorously and refrigerate. Will keep for one month. Shake well before using.

Basting Sauce for Meats

Meats are basted with this sauce for more flavor and so that they will brown when roasted in the microwave oven. This basting sauce can be used with all meats and poultry.

1 tbsp. (15 mL) vegetable oil or unsalted margarine or butter, (melted 1 minute at HIGH)

1 tsp. (5 mL) paprika

1 tsp. (5 mL) Kitchen Bouquet

1/4 tsp. (1 mL) thyme, tarragon, basil, marjoram, cumin or curry

Stir all ingredients together and brush mixture all over meat before cooking.

Aromatics for basting meats

Use the aromatic of your choice for basting meats before and during their cooking to enhance their flavor and to brown them.

Ready basting for beef

2 tbsp. (30 mL) Madeira or whisky or cold tea

or

1 tsp. (5 mL) tomato paste *and*
3 tsp. (15 mL) water

or

4 tbsp. (60 mL) canned consommé, undiluted

Heat the aromatic of your choice 30 seconds at HIGH. Use to baste meat before and during cooking.

Breaded Veal Chops (p. 53) →

Ready basting for pork

Rind and juice of half an orange

or

1/4 cup (60 mL) cranberry juice mixed with
1 tsp. (5 mL) cornstarch

or

3 tbsp. (50 mL) water *and*
2 tsp. (10 mL) instant coffee

Heat the aromatic of your choice 30 seconds at HIGH. Use to baste meat before and during cooking.

Ready basting for veal

3 tbsp. (50 mL) white wine or dry sherry

or

1 tbsp. (15 mL) soy sauce (preferably
Japanese)

or

2 tbsp. (30 mL) Teriyaki sauce (bottled)

or

2 tsp. (10 mL) Worcestershire sauce

or

2 tbsp. (30 mL) sour cream

Add 1 tsp. (5 mL) paprika to the aromatic of your choice. Heat 30 seconds at HIGH. Mix well and baste meat with it before and during cooking.

Ready basting for lamb

2 to 3 tbsp. (30 to 50 mL) Madeira

or

1 tbsp. (15 mL) mint sauce (not jelly)

or

2 tsp. (10 mL) instant coffee *and*

3 tbsp. (50 mL) water

or

juice and rind of half a lemon *and*
1/2 tsp. (2 mL) fresh grated ginger

Heat the aromatic of your choice 30 seconds at HIGH. Use to baste meat before and during cooking.

Sauce Vaucluse

2 tbsp. (30 mL) butter
2 tbsp. (30 mL) flour
1½ cups (375 mL) cream

salt and pepper to taste
2 egg yolks, beaten
1 recipe of Hollandaise sauce

Melt the butter 1 minute at HIGH. Add the flour and mix well. Add the cream and stir. Cook 3 to 4 minutes at HIGH, stirring a few times, until sauce is creamy. Add the beaten egg yolks, stirring constantly, then add the Hollandaise while stirring, until sauce is smooth and creamy.
To reheat, place the sauce in the oven 1 minute at HIGH, stir well and if necessary heat 30 seconds more at MEDIUM-HIGH. Stir and serve.

←Top: Honey-glazed Half Ham (p. 83)
←Bottom: Short Beef Ribs, Barbecued (p. 40)

Meat Tenderizer Marinating Sauce

Less tender meat cuts such as shoulder, brisket, heel of round, stewing beef, will become tender after marinating in this mixture.

2/3 cup (160 mL) onion, chopped fine

3/4 cup (200 mL) celery leaves, minced

1/3 cup (80 mL) cider vinegar

1/2 cup (125 mL) vegetable oil

1 cup (250 mL) grape juice

1 tbsp. (15 mL) hot sauce

1/2 tsp. (2 mL) salt

1/8 tsp. (0.5 mL) powdered garlic

Combine all the ingredients together and mix well. Pour over the meat cut to be marinated, covering it. Refrigerate 12 to 24 hours.

To roast the meat, drain from the marinade. Cook following your recipe. Baste the roast 2 to 3 times with the marinating sauce during the cooking.

Applesauce

It is delicious with pork or ham.

4 - 5 apples, quartered

4 tbsp. (60 mL) water

2 tbsp. (30 mL) butter

Peel the apples and quarter, place them in a baking dish and add water. Cover and cook 5 minutes at HIGH. Remove from oven, pass through a sieve or use a food processor. Place in the oven 1 minute at HIGH. Add the butter, stir well until the butter has melted. Do not sweeten.

True Hollandaise

A sheer delight to make. Never fails.

1/3 to 1/2 cup (80 to 125 mL) salted or
   unsalted butter

2 egg yolks

juice of one small lemon

Place the butter in a small casserole or a 2-cup (500 mL) measure. Heat, uncovered, 1 minute at MEDIUM-HIGH. Add egg yolks and lemon juice. Beat well with a small whisk. Cook 20 seconds at MEDIUM-HIGH, beat well and if necessary cook 20 seconds more at MEDIUM-HIGH, for the sauce to have a creamy texture. Whisk, salt to taste and serve.

My Favorite Tomato Sauce

Serve it with veal or pork, or with leftover meat thinly sliced, cover with the sauce, heat and serve.

3 slices bacon, diced

1 large onion, minced

1 tbsp. (15 mL) flour

4 large fresh tomatoes

1/8 tsp. (0.5 mL) nutmeg

1/2 tsp. (2 mL) thyme

1/2 tsp. (2 mL) salt

1/2 cup (125 mL) tomato paste

1 tsp. (5 mL) sugar

Place the bacon in a 4-cup (1 L) bowl, cover with waxed paper. Cook 2 minutes at HIGH. Remove diced bacon from fat and drain; let cool. To the fat remaining, add the onion, stir and cook 4 minutes at HIGH, stirring halfway through the cooking. Add the flour and mix well, add the remaining ingredients. Stir to blend. Cover and cook 5 minutes at HIGH, stirring twice. Taste for seasoning. Add the bacon and stir well.

This sauce will keep one week if refrigerated in a glass jar. To reheat, pour into a bowl and heat 2-3 minutes at HIGH.

Raisin Sauce

A sweet sauce traditionally served with ham, small tongues or veal.

1/2 cup (125 mL) brown sugar

1 tbsp. (15 mL) cornstarch

1 tsp. (5 mL) dry mustard

2 tbsp. (30 mL) cider vinegar

2 tbsp. (30 mL) lemon juice

rind of half a lemon, not grated

1½ cups (375 mL) water

1/3 cup (80 mL) seedless raisins

1 tbsp. (15 mL) butter

In a 4-cup (1 L) measure, combine all ingredients, stirring until thoroughly mixed. Cook, uncovered, 4 minutes at HIGH. Stir and cook 1 or 2 minutes more if necessary.

How to thicken a sauce

To the fat in the pan or the plate, add 2 tbsp. (30 mL) flour before adding the liquid. Blend well. Add the cold water or tea, or the port wine or vodka or white vermouth or red wine. Stir scratching the bottom of the pan. Cook 2 minutes at HIGH. Stir until the sauce is creamy.

Barbecue Sauce

This sauce will keep 10 days refrigerated or two months frozen.

3 tbsp. (50 mL) vegetable oil or olive oil

1 envelope onion soup mix

1/2 cup (125 mL) diced celery

3/4 cup (200 mL) chili sauce or ketchup

1/4 cup (60 mL) tomato juice, red wine
or water

1/4 tsp. (1 mL) celery seeds

1/4 cup (60 mL) cider vinegar

1/4 cup (60 mL) well-packed brown sugar

1 tbsp. (15 mL) Dijon mustard

grated rind of 1 orange, 1 lemon

Place oil and onion soup mix in a 6-cup (1.5 L) casserole. Stir well and cook 1 minute at HIGH. Add all the remaining ingredients, stir well. Cook 4 minutes at HIGH, or until sauce bubbles. Stir well. If you wish to refrigerate or freeze sauce, cool first.

Sauce Aurore

Serve with veal.

3 tbsp. (50 mL) butter

3 tbsp. (50 mL) flour

2 cups (500 mL) milk or chicken broth

1/2 cup (125 mL) whipping cream

salt and pepper to taste

3 tbsp. (50 mL) tomato paste

1 tsp. (5 mL) basil

3 tbsp. (50 mL) parsley, minced

1 tbsp. (15 mL) soft butter

Melt the butter 1 minute at HIGH. Add the flour and stir well. Add the milk or chicken broth, stir well. Cook 4 minutes at HIGH. Stir well. When the sauce is smooth and creamy, gradually add the cream, stirring constantly. Salt and pepper to taste. Add the tomato paste, basil and parsley. Mix thoroughly. Cook 2 minutes at HIGH. Stir well, if necessary cook another 2 minutes at HIGH, or until the sauce is creamy. Add the soft butter, stir to melt the butter. Do not reheat the sauce after adding the tablespoon (15 mL) of butter.

The Finishing Touch
— Buttering a sauce

The French chef's method of finishing a sauce is to add butter to the sauce as soon as it is cooked and to stir until the butter is melted. The heat of the completed sauce melts the butter; it is not necessary to return it to the oven. This is called "buttering a sauce".

Hollandaise Sauce in the Food Processor

The Hollandaise prepared in this manner will keep refrigerated, for 2 to 3 days. Use it cold over steaks garnished with avocado or over thin slices of veal. This sauce is easily reheated, 30 seconds to 1 minute at MEDIUM; stir well after 30 seconds and heat another 20 to 30 seconds, if necessary.

1/2 cup (125 mL) cold butter
2 tbsp. (30 mL) lemon or lime juice
1/2 tsp. (2 mL) Dijon mustard

1/8 tsp. (.05 mL) pepper
2 egg yolks at room temperature

Dice the butter and place in the food processor bowl without the metal blade. Place the bowl in the microwave oven and heat at HIGH 30 seconds to 1 minute, the butter must not melt but only soften. Return the bowl to the food processor, insert the blade, add the lemon or lime juice, mustard and pepper. Cover and operate 2 seconds or until the mixture is creamy. Without stopping the motor, add the egg yolks through the tube, 1 at a time, blending 30 seconds after each yolk addition.
Uncover, remove the blade and cook at MEDIUM approximately 1 minute. Stir, and cook another 20 seconds if necessary. Serve, or refrigerate in a well-covered container.
The explanation is rather lengthy, but the process is easy.

Hollandaise Variations

Sauce Mousseline
Add to the Hollandaise of your choice 2 egg whites beaten stiff. For the sauce to be light and fluffy, add the egg whites immediately before serving.

De Luxe mustard sauce
In the Hollandaise of your choice, replace the lemon juice by 2 tablespoons (30 mL) of cold water and 1 tablespoon (15 mL) of Dijon mustard. Mix well.

Sauce Maltaise
In the Hollandaise of your choice, replace the lemon juice by 4 tablespoons (60 mL) of the juice and grated rind of one orange.

Chantilly Hollandaise

1 recipe of Hollandaise sauce
1/2 cup (125 mL) whipping cream

Prepare the Hollandaise of your choice. Immediately before serving, whip the cream and beat it into the sauce.
This sauce is served warm, as it would not remain fluffy if reheated and it could curdle.

Herb Butter

Prepare this butter which may be kept one month in the refrigerator and 12 months in the freezer. Shape the butter into small balls, place them in a box with a tight lid if you wish to refrigerate them. To freeze, cool the butter balls one hour, then spread out on a cookie sheet and freeze; this may take 3 to 4 hours. Then place the balls in a freezer bag. To serve, just drop a butter ball over each serving.

1 cup (250 mL) unsalted butter*

1 tsp. (5 mL) dill

1/2 tsp. (2 mL) tarragon

1/2 tsp. (2 mL) savory

1/4 cup (60 mL) chopped parsley

4 green onions, chopped fine, the white and the green

1 tsp. (5 mL) powdered coriander (optional)

1 tsp. (5 mL) salt

1/4 tsp. (1 mL) fresh ground pepper

grated rind of half a lemon

Cream all the ingredients together, cool one hour in the refrigerator. Shape into small balls and refrigerate or freeze, as you wish.

* If you use salted butter, reduce the salt called for in the recipe to 1/4 tsp. (1 mL).

Green Sauce

A delicious classic sauce to serve with all boiled meats. It is served cold on hot meat; it is in a sense a French dressing. It may be kept from 4 to 6 weeks refrigerated in a glass jar. To serve, let oil warm up 3 to 4 hours at room temperature.

1 onion, peeled and grated

or

6 green onions, minced

3 tbsp. (50 mL) parsley, finely minced

1 tbsp. (15 mL) marinated capers

1 garlic clove, crushed

1 tbsp. (15 mL) fine breadcrumbs

4 to 5 tbsp. (60 to 75 mL) vegetable oil

the juice and rind of 1 lemon

salt and pepper to taste

Place in a bowl the grated onion or the green onions, parsley, capers, garlic and breadcrumbs. Mix well. Add the oil and lemon juice and rind, stirring constantly. Salt and pepper to taste.

Reducing a sauce with no starch

A sauce is reduced to give it a more concentrated flavor, as well as to thicken it.
Boil the sauce at HIGH one minute at a time, stirring well each time, until you reach the desired consistency.

Sauce Béarnaise

A Béarnaise is a Hollandaise seasoned with tarragon and white wine vinegar. It is the ideal sauce to serve with broiled steak.

3 tbsp. (50 mL) white wine or cider vinegar

1 green onion, chopped

1 tsp. (5 mL) tarragon

4 peppercorns, ground

1/3 cup (80 mL) butter

2 egg yolks, beaten

Place the vinegar, onion and tarragon in a 2-cup (500 mL) measure. Heat, uncovered, 2 minutes at HIGH. Put through a sieve into an attractive microwave ovenware dish, pressing the onions. Add the ground peppercorns and butter. Melt 1 minute at HIGH. Add the beaten egg yolks. Cook, uncovered, 30 seconds at HIGH, beat well and cook 20 seconds more, or until the sauce is creamy.

Raisin Sauce for Ham

It is delicious served with boiled or braised ham. This sauce will keep 3 to 4 days, cooked and refrigerated.

1/2 cup (125 mL) brown sugar

2 tbsp. (30 mL) cornstarch

1 tsp. (5 mL) dry mustard

2 tbsp. (30 mL) cider vinegar

2 tbsp. (30 mL) lemon juice

grated rind of half a lemon

1½ cups (375 mL) water

1/3 cup (80 mL) seedless raisins

1 tbsp. (15 mL) butter

Combine all the ingredients together in a 4-cup (1 L) measure. Cook, uncovered, 3 to 4 minutes at HIGH, stirring twice during the cooking. If necessary, continue to cook 1 minute at a time until the sauce is light and creamy.

Sour Cream Sauce

Flavorful, creamy and easy to prepare, this sauce is the perfect accompaniment to veal, poultry and vegetables.

1 cup (225 mL) sour cream

1/2 tsp. (2 mL) salt

1/2 tsp. (2 mL) curry

1/8 tsp. (0.5 mL) pepper

1 tbsp. (15 mL) lemon juice

grated rind of 1 lemon

Combine all the ingredients together in a 2-cup (500 mL) measure. Cook, uncovered, 2 minutes at MEDIUM-HIGH, stirring twice during the cooking. If necessary, cook one minute more.

Gravy without starch

Add to the "fumet" in the pan or the plate 1/4 cup (60 mL) cold tea or water, or port wine or vodka or white vermouth or red wine or dry Madeira, stir with a wooden spoon scratching the bottom of the pan or plate. Cook 1 minute at HIGH and serve.

Onion Butter for Steak

I always keep some of this butter in my refrigerator, to put on microwave broiled steaks, hamburgers, sausages or chicken. The heat of the meat melts the butter.

4 tbsp. (60 mL) grated onion

4 tbsp. (60 mL) minced parsley

4 tbsp. (60 mL) soft butter

1 tsp. (5 mL) A-1 Sauce or chutney

1/2 tsp. (2 mL) salt

1/4 tsp. (1 mL) dry mustard

1/2 tsp. (2 mL) fresh ground pepper

Mix all the ingredients together. Place in a container or form into small balls, place them on a baking sheet and freeze uncovered, for about one hour. When they are frozen, place the butter balls in a plastic box with a sheet of waxed paper between the rows. Keep in the refrigerator or in the freezer. Even when frozen the butter melts when placed on the hot meat.

Sauce Ravigote

This sauce may be served with roasted or boiled beef, spare-ribs, or to reheat leftover meat.

4 green onions, chopped, the green and the white

3 tbsp. (50 mL) wine vinegar

1/3 cup (80 mL) parsley, chopped fine

1 tbsp. (15 mL) tarragon

1¼ cups (300 mL) broth of your choice

1 tbsp. (15 mL) butter

1 tbsp. (15 mL) flour

1 egg yolk

salt and pepper to taste

Place in a measuring cup the onions and the wine vinegar. Cook 2 to 3 minutes at HIGH, or until there is but one spoonful of vinegar left. Pass through a sieve and pour the juice into the broth. Add the parsley and tarragon.

Place the butter and flour in a bowl. Cook 1 minute at HIGH, stir well and keep on cooking one minute at a time, stirring after each minute, until the sauce browns lightly.

Pour into the broth, mix well and cook 2 minutes at HIGH, stirring after 1 minute. Taste for seasoning. This sauce is slightly thickened.

This sauce may also be prepared by replacing the ground pepper with 4 black peppercorns coarsely ground and 1 tablespoon (15 mL) of cognac or white wine.

White Vermouth Sauce

This is one of my favorites. It is quickly prepared, it enhances the flavor of kidneys and calves' brains, and is perfect for reheating thin slices of leftover beef or veal.

2 tbsp. (30 mL) vegetable oil

1 medium onion, chopped fine

1 French shallot, chopped fine

1 tbsp. (15 mL) flour

2 tsp. (10 mL) tomato paste

1/3 cup (80 mL) dry white vermouth

1 cup (250 mL) beef broth

1 tbsp. (15 mL) lemon juice

1/4 tsp. (1 mL) sugar

salt and pepper to taste

Heat the oil in a 4-cup measure (1 L) 1 minute at HIGH. Add the onion and shallot, mix well and cook 2 minutes at HIGH. Stir in the flour and tomato paste. Mix well, add the vermouth and beef broth. Beat with a wire whisk. Cook 4 minutes at MEDIUM-HIGH, stirring halfway through the cooking. Add the lemon juice and the sugar, beat well and cook 1 minute at HIGH. Salt and pepper to taste. Serve.
This sauce reheats very well at MEDIUM-HIGH.

White Wine Mushroom Sauce

Serve with veal or pork. Excellent with leftover meat, diced or thinly sliced and covered with this sauce, and only 2 minutes at HIGH when ready to serve. Serve with Rice Pilaff.

1 tbsp. (15 mL) butter

1 cup (250 mL), very full, thinly sliced mushrooms

2 French shallots or 4 green onions

1 tbsp. (15 mL) cornstarch

1/2 cup (125 mL) white wine or juice of half a lemon

1 tbsp. (15 mL) cream

salt and pepper to taste

Melt the butter in a 4-cup (1 L) measure 1 minute at HIGH. Add the washed mushrooms, thinly sliced. Finely chop the shallots or green onions. Add to the mushrooms together with the cornstarch, mix well. Cook 2 minutes at HIGH. Stir. Add the white wine or the lemon juice, cream, salt and pepper to taste, and cook 2 minutes more at HIGH, stirring halfway through the cooking. This sauce reheats well, 2 minutes at MEDIUM.

Timbale Mushroom Sauce

A recipe to use whenever you wish to serve a mushroom sauce. The color will vary from light beige to golden brown depending on whether you use dry Madeira or soy sauce, and the flavor will also vary. Both are good.

3 tbsp. (50 mL) butter or margarine

2 tbsp. (30 mL) flour

1 tsp. (5 mL) soy sauce *or*

1 tbsp. (15 mL) dry Madeira

3/4 cup (200 mL) light cream or milk

1/4 tsp. (1 mL) salt

A 4 oz. (112 g) can chopped mushrooms, undrained

1/4 tsp. (1 mL) tarragon or curry powder

Place butter in a 4-cup (1 L) glass bowl. Heat 1 minute at HIGH. To the melted butter, add the flour, soy sauce, or dry Madeira. Blend to a smooth paste. Add cream or milk, stir until smooth. Add salt, mushrooms, tarragon or curry powder. Cook, uncovered, 2 minutes at HIGH. Stir well. Cook another minute. Stir well. By this time sauce should be thick and creamy. If it gets cold before you are ready to serve, stir well, heat 1 minute at HIGH, uncovered.

My Barbecue Sauce

Through the years, I have made many a barbecue sauce. This one has remained my favorite. It can be used with pork, beef, lamb, or poultry. When cooled, place in glass jar, cover and refrigerate. It will keep 2 to 3 weeks.

1/2 cup (125 mL) dark brown sugar

1 tbsp. (15 mL) cornstarch

1 tsp. (5 mL) curry or chili powder

An 8-oz. (250 mL) can tomato sauce

1/2 cup (125 mL) cider or wine vinegar

1/2 cup (125 mL) chili sauce or ketchup

1/2 cup (125 mL) corn syrup

1/2 cup (125 mL) cold water

1/4 cup (60 mL) rum or orange liqueur

In a large measuring cup place the brown sugar, cornstarch, curry or chili powder. Stir to mix. Add the tomato sauce, vinegar, chili sauce or ketchup, corn syrup and cold water. Stir to mix. Cook, uncovered, at HIGH for 10 minutes. Stir well, add the rum or orange liqueur. Cook 3 minutes at MEDIUM. Stir. Pour into a glass jar. Cover, use, or refrigerate.

Index

Printed by
PAYETTE & SIMMS, INC.
in February, 1987
at Saint-Lambert, Qué.